abstract painting

FOR THE ABSOLUTE BEGINNER

Book Cover Design by
Ruth Anna Evans

Edited by
Tasha Reynolds

All artwork in this book created by Lori Rivera.

www.loririveraart.com

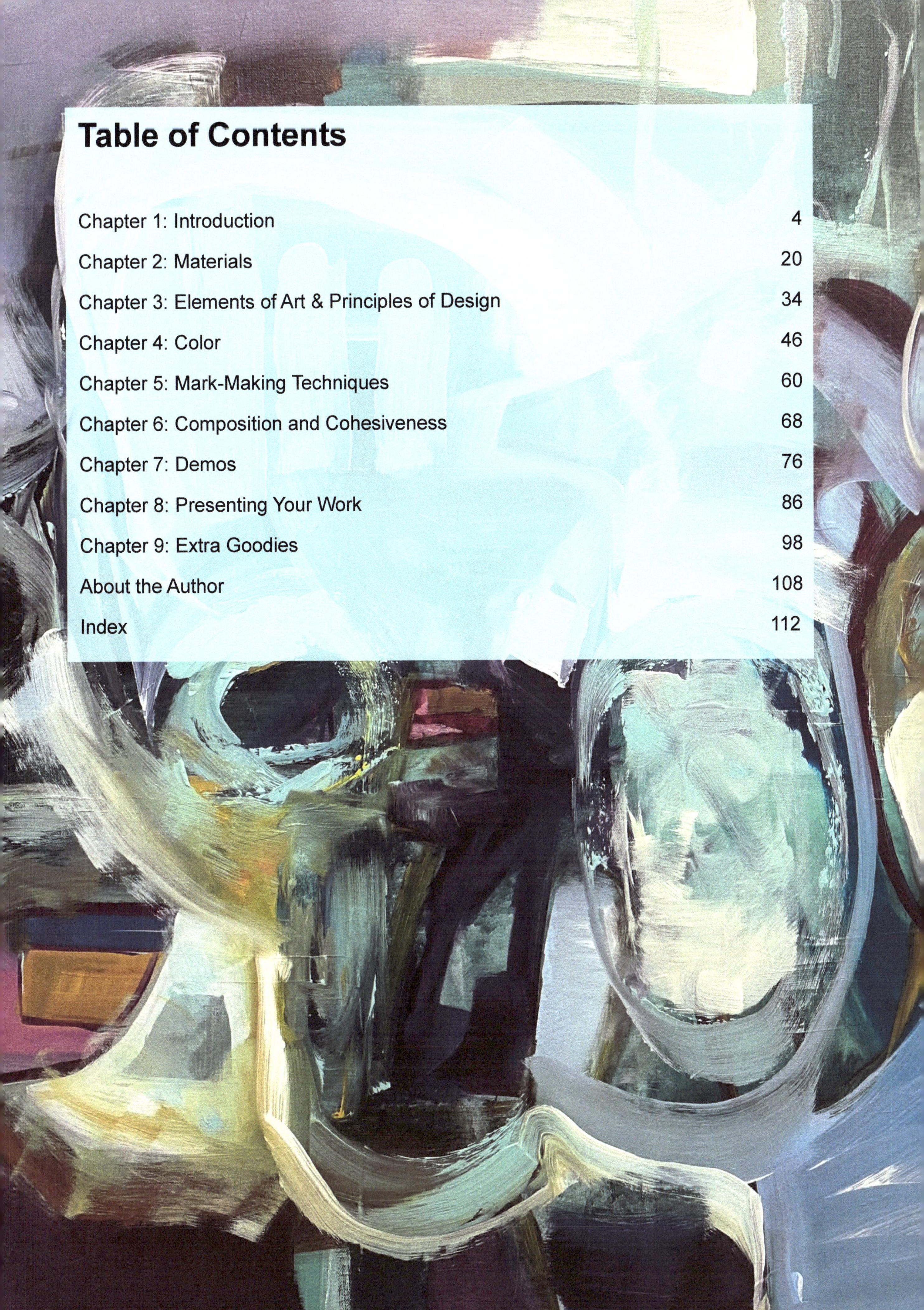

Table of Contents

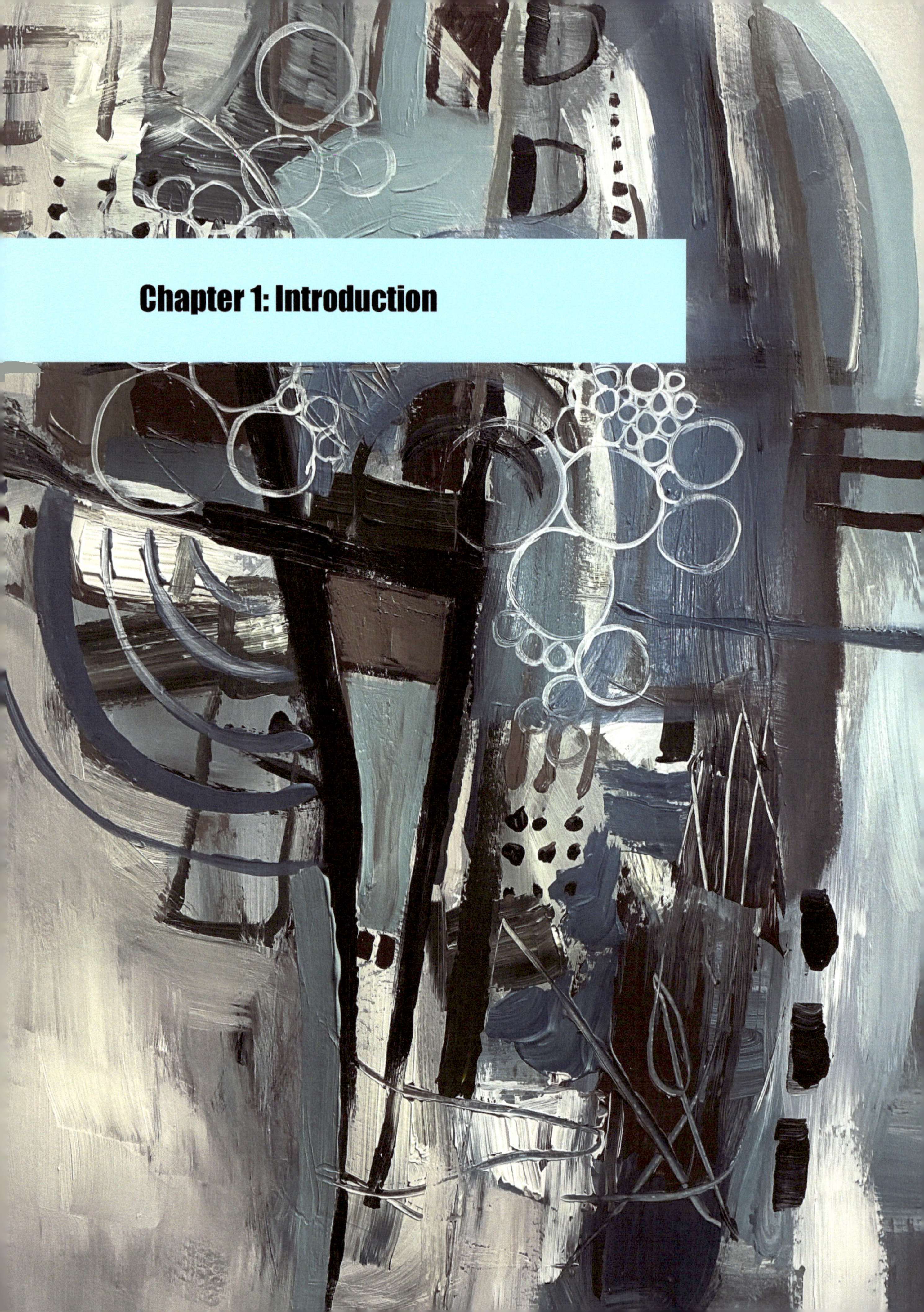

Chapter 1: Introduction

Introduction

I'm glad you found your way to this book, my fellow creative. I'm excited to share the experience of abstract painting with you and I'm honored that you trust me to introduce you to abstract painting.

I always took art classes in school growing up but didn't fully commit myself to painting until I was an adult. While working for a nonprofit peer mental health recovery center, I had the opportunity to take some art classes under a grant we received. A couple years later I left my job to focus on my art career, and I've been painting ever since. I've written this book based on my experience. I've sold over 250 paintings (about a third abstracts) and have been running my art business professionally since the beginning of 2021.

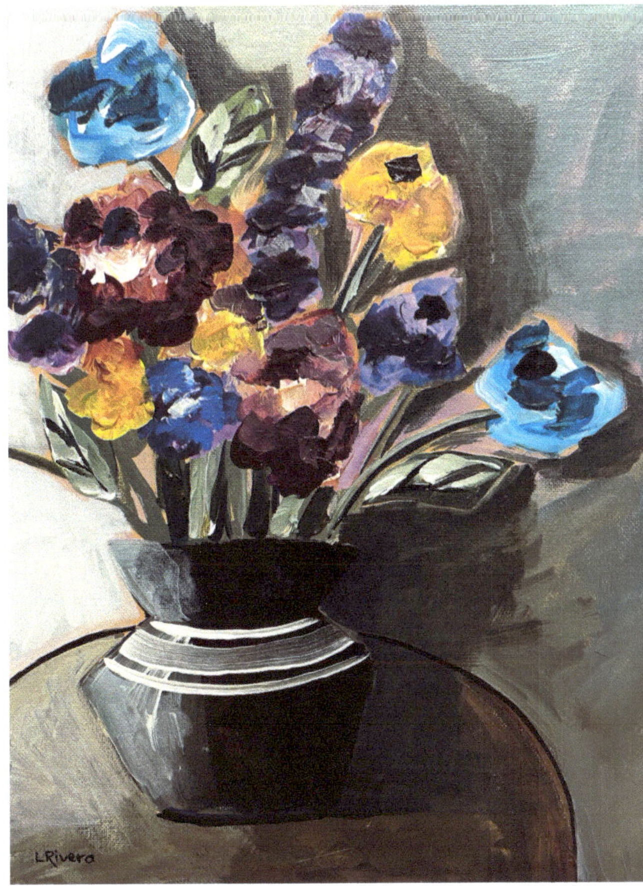

Spring Joy
14x11 acrylic on canvas panel

Abstraction really lies on a continuum. I consider the piece at the top right to be an abstracted still life. At the other end of the spectrum, on the bottom right is one of my nonrepresentational abstract pieces. There are many levels of abstraction in between these two examples. Nonrepresentational (or nonobjective) simply means that the painting doesn't represent an object from reality.

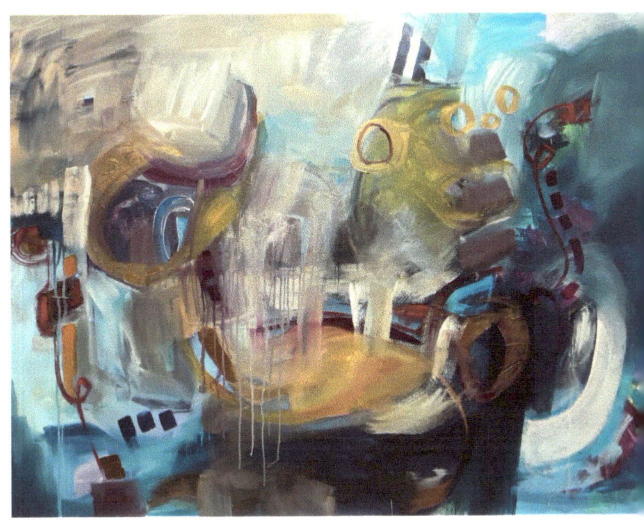

Change of Plans
36x48 acrylic on canvas

Creating something from nearly nothing except your intuition, imagination, and emotions with just tubes of paint and paper or a blank canvas can be intimidating, but I'm going to give you the knowledge you need to get started. What will help you the most, though, is actual practice. The only way to get better at something is to do it often, so paint as often as you possibly can.

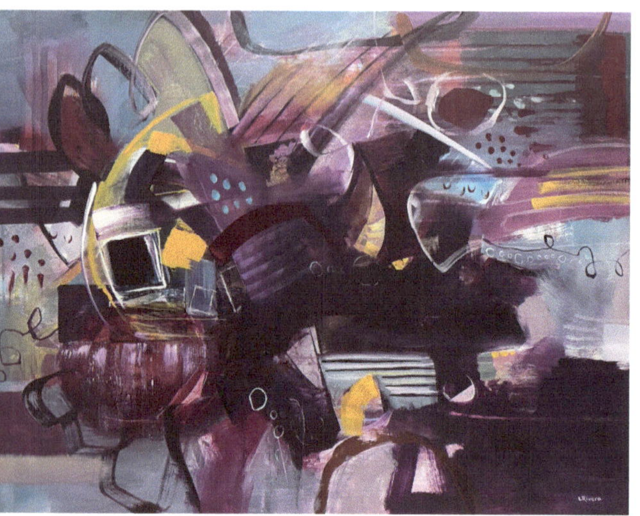

Kinetic
30x40 acrylic on canvas

There are several things you need to do to be successful at abstract painting. First, you have to overcome the fear of painting abstracts. You can't be afraid of disappointment, of trying new things, or of simply what transpires on the canvas.

You also must be comfortable with the fact that you will have a lot of experimenting and practicing to do (unless you have an innate ability to paint abstracts, which is possible). You have to be okay with being a beginner. Just like anything else, good abstracts come with practice - an enormous amount of practice. But painting abstracts can be the most relaxing, challenging, and rewarding activity, if you allow it to be.

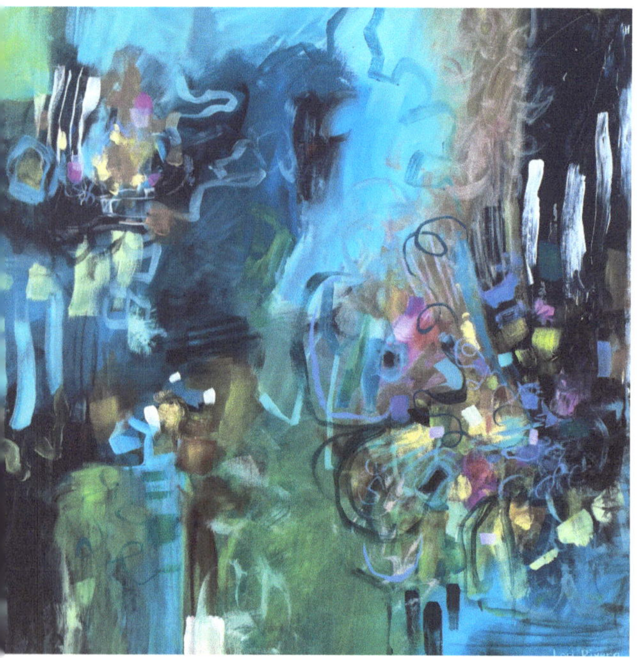

Lush Vegetation
24x24 acrylic on canvas

Even after you read this book, your success will ultimately depend on your dedication to your painting practice. There's no guarantee you'll be able to create pieces you are happy with right away because it takes a lot of experimenting and hard work, but my hope is that this book will give you a big boost.

You also must work through the ugly stages. By nature, many abstract paintings go through stages when you paint them, and somewhere in the middle it's possible your pieces won't be visually striking. As a matter of fact, they may look like a huge mess. I used to be guilty of quitting when my paintings were in these stages and I had to learn to work through them. This is the only way you will be able to get really good at painting abstracts. I can't say it enough. You have to work through the awkward and ugly stages; you have to give your paintings time to develop, and this might involve layer after layer of paint.

As you look through the demos in Chapter Seven, you'll see that many times I start out with dark colors, and then move to lighter ones. Lately that hasn't been the case though. My goal is always to transform that beginning mess into something beautiful, moving, or both.

I'm still evolving in my painting journey, even after over five years of being fully committed to painting. I still learn every day and my work continually changes. It may take some time, but with lots of practice, working through the different stages of your pieces, and never giving up, you'll begin to create some really nice pieces of abstract art.

To give you a frame of reference, at the top right is one of my first abstract paintings, and the one below it is a recent abstract. My early abstracts look much different than my current ones. You'll find that your style will evolve as well.

Abstract painting is a journey that will keep you energized, excited, and inspired for years to come. Abstract art has provided an essential outlet for me to express myself, provides a way to manage my mental health, and brings happiness to others. My abstract work tends to be on the vibrant and cheerful side most often.

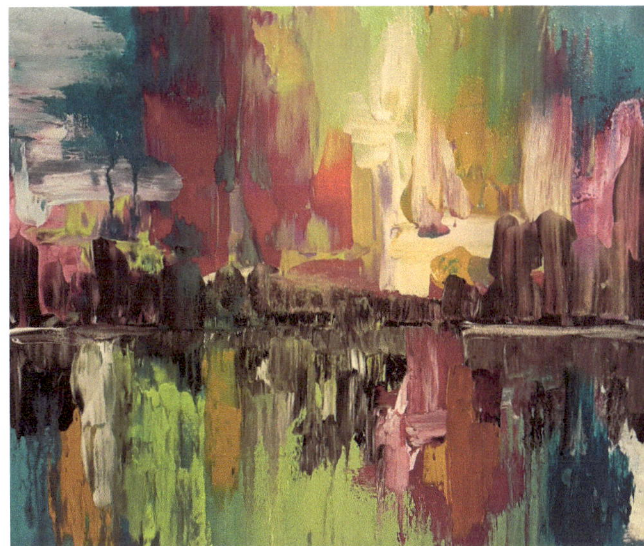

Fragmentations
11x14 acrylic on wood

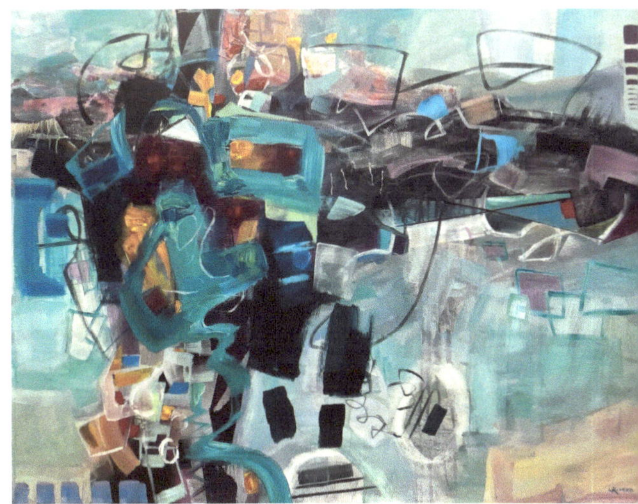

Buzzing with Anticipation
30x40 acrylic on canvas

“It took me four years to paint like Raphael, but a lifetime to paint like a child.” - Picasso

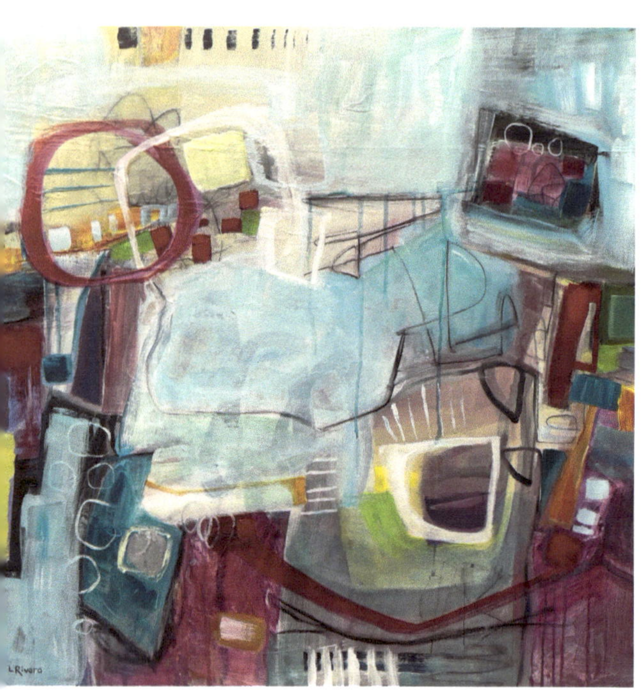

Don’t Stop Thinking About Tomorrow
24x24 acrylic on canvas

Consider Why You Love Abstraction

One thing I want you to think about is why you love abstract art. You really should know why you like it before you start painting. This will give you a sense of purpose and motivation for creating. It could simply be that abstract paintings move you, that you love the beauty, tension, or darkness of the pieces, or something else individual to you. But I do want you to think about why you love to paint, because that will help direct you in your painting practice.

As the Picasso quote to the left implies, it’s difficult to paint as playfully and free as a child when we reach adulthood. Young children are not afraid to express themselves through art because they don’t have societal expectations holding them back yet. But somewhere along the way, we develop filters through which our art is subjected. We must ignore these filters that tell us what is good art and what is bad art. We need to recapture our childhood fearlessness and be able to create for the sake of creating. Work created under this intention can be the best.

Furthermore, I believe we are constricted by how the world around us is made up of definite objects and finite designs. All of this is very limiting and influences us, many times unknowingly, into creating art a certain way. We must move beyond that, and embrace the freedom to abstract. It also helps when we learn to notice and appreciate abstraction in everyday life, in everything from architecture to clothing.

I think there’s a general belief that the more realistic the artwork looks, the better it is. Many look at abstract work and compare it to child's play. But I doubt the ones who think this way have ever tried to paint abstractly, if at all. If they did, they'd realize how challenging it is to create a good abstract composition and use just the right colors that sing together.

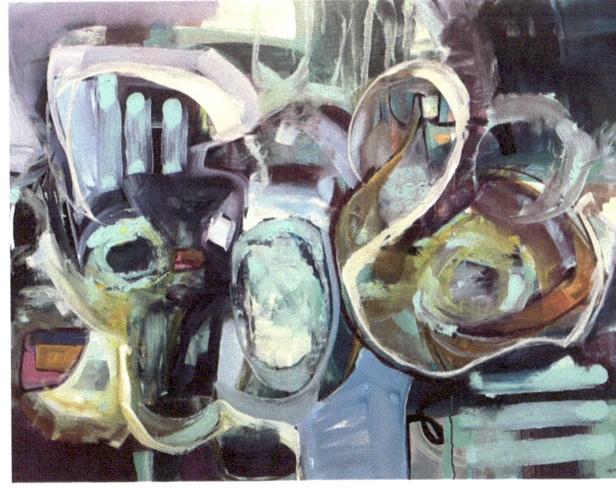

There's No Turnin' Back
36x48 acrylic on canvas

I find I'm still learning how to make good abstract art each time I paint. I never stop learning and my goal is to learn and grow with every piece I create.

Abstract art serves many functions, and is often the choice of decor in hospitals and many other businesses. Nonobjective abstract work is very neutral, meaning usually it can't be interpreted as being religious, political, or offensive in any way.

Something else that excites me to paint abstracts is that I find abstract art to be the most challenging to create. Abstract art that has depth, movement, good value contrast, and good composition is hard to create. Sometimes it takes me longer to create a good abstract painting than it does for me to create a fairly detailed still life painting. For someone else, the opposite might true. For me, however, abstract pieces are the most challenging. Furthermore, on some days abstracts flow just right, while other times nothing I paint is exactly the way I want it to look.

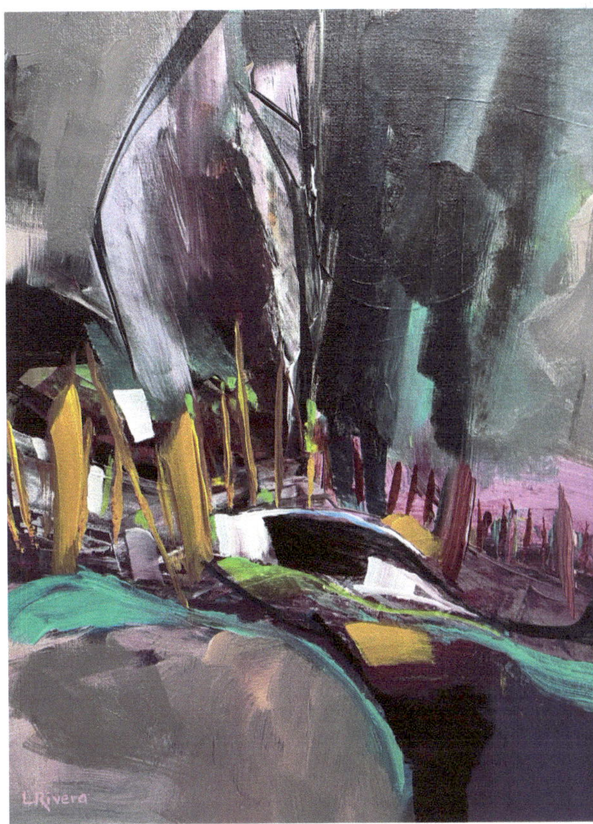

Emergence of Spring
14x11 acrylic on canvas panel

"Sometimes the bravest and most important thing you can do is just show up." - Brené Brown

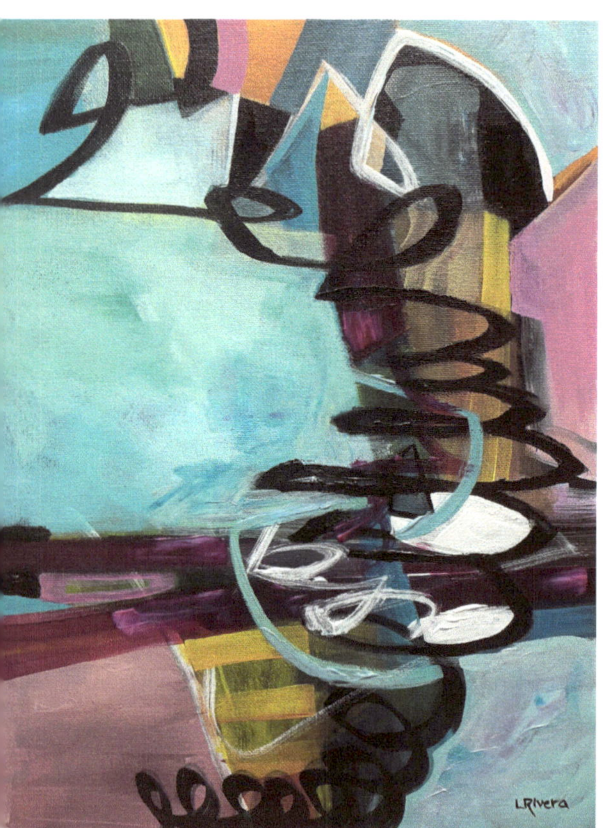

Treasured Spaces
14x11 acrylic on canvas panel

Showing Up, Even When Not Inspired

I love the quote of Brené Brown's to the left. This is how I feel about the painting process, as when I go for several days without spending time in my studio, I feel as though my flow has been interrupted. In painting, and in life, I believe that showing up is half the battle. I try to paint daily, but if for some reason I can't paint, I try to organize and clean my studio instead. Just spending time in my studio is so important.

Having the motivation to step into my studio is the biggest, but most important hurdle. Sometimes I might not be in the mood to paint, but if I show up and spend some time in my studio, many times looking at other paintings I've finished will spark ideas for new paintings. Sometimes it's just a matter of taking a painting I am not completely happy with and totally painting over it - or just adding some new layers. Some of my best ideas come out of simply spending time in the studio. Being in there with no pressure to produce allows me to relax and let my mind wander.

Sometimes I just look through art magazines or books for inspiration. This is really just as important as the painting process itself. Allowing my brain to soak in everything helps me gear up for my next painting session, and I really think that like most artists, I desire a lot of visual stimulation and absorb all of it around me.

Sometimes when I don't feel inspired to paint, I try to go in my studio to paint anyway. To me, the act of painting is just as important as the end result of a painting. Many times this is when I really pour my emotions onto the canvas. When this happens, sometimes something beautiful surfaces, but other times the outcome isn't so pretty. My mantra is, "*If you don't like it, just paint over it.*" That's the beauty of acrylic.

Another thing I have discovered is that if I'm not feeling inspired to paint, that is a perfect time to paint a still life — where my subject is fairly easily decided, and I can focus on improving my technical painting skills rather than relying on my imagination to paint an abstract.

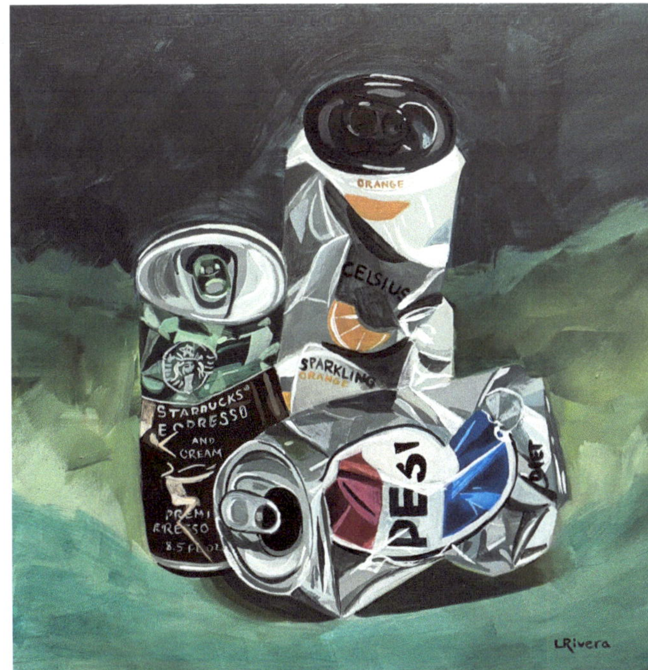

Three Moods
10x10 acrylic on cradled wood panel

Creative Process

It used to be that I'd have five or more in-progress paintings and I'd bounce back and forth between them. What I found to be true, for me anyway, is that I was not finishing many pieces of art. This was also a time when I did not have enough experience to know that abstract paintings can go through many ugly stages before they become nice pieces. I'd have tons of paintings in progress that honestly were all in ugly stages. I would abandon each piece during an awkward stage and never return to it.

A couple of years ago, I had an intentional plan to not start any new pieces until I finished the one I was currently working on. Surprisingly, I found this approach to painting more fitting for me, even though it was not easy to change my creative routine. Not only was I able to finish paintings, but my painting itself seemed to improve.

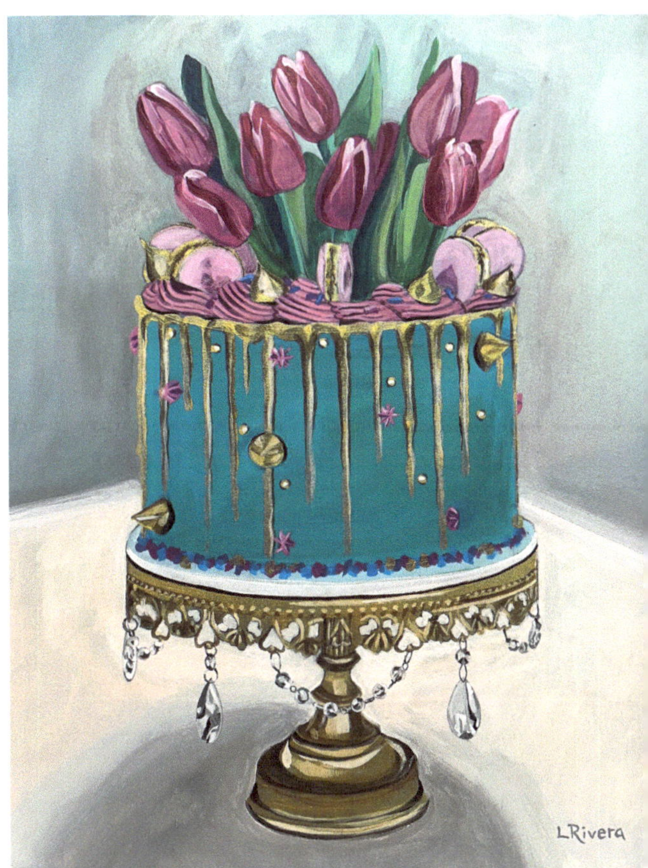

Celebration Cake
14x11 acrylic on cradled wood panel

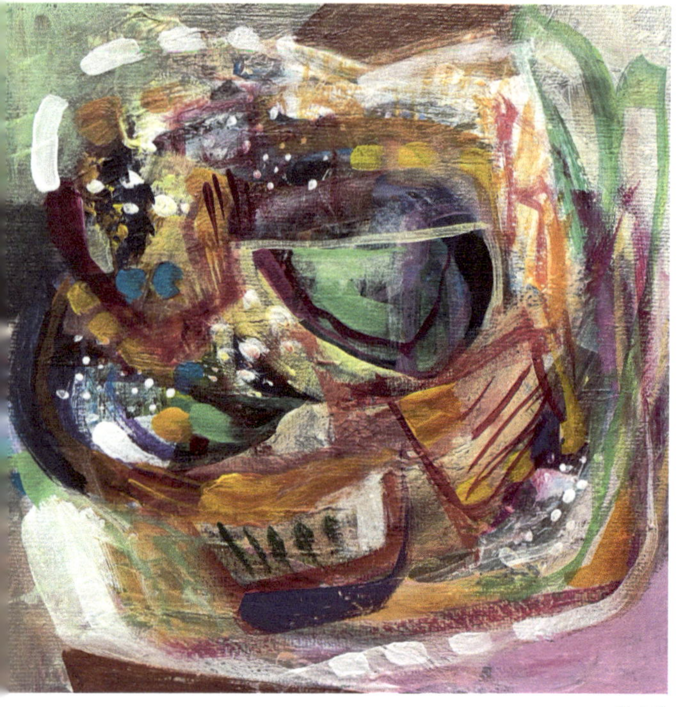

Orbit
6x6 acrylic on canvas panel

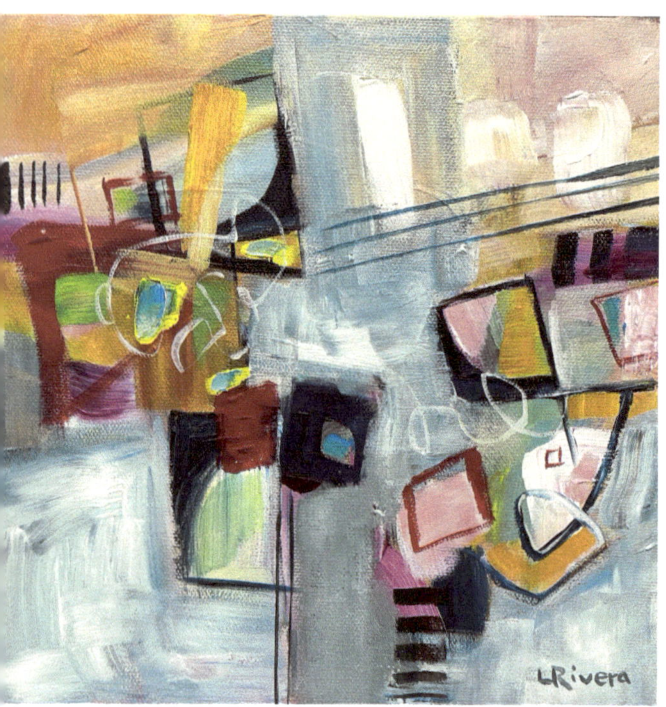

Leave It All Behind
10x10 acrylic on canvas

I know this method of finishing one painting at a time isn't a good fit for everyone, but it seems to work for me. I do stay open to going back to my old method of having several in-progress paintings at the same time, though sometimes I think just changing our creative process or routine a little can spark interesting changes in our work. I should add here that I usually have multiple projects going on at once. I may only have one abstract I'm working on, but I usually have a still life or something else I'm working on while the layers of my abstract dry.

There's a huge sense of accomplishment with each finished piece. Starting and finishing one piece at a time (knowing I can't start a new one until I finish my current one) provides the motivation needed to finish the piece. This motivation also forces me to work through all the stages instead of putting the piece aside when the going gets tough.

What Helped Me Get to Where I am Today

I think it's important to share how I've arrived at where I am today. The following is what I think were the most important things that helped me grow as an artist.

Creating Daily

First, if you can, create art daily. Even if it's just for a half an hour, that is better than nothing. When you do this, you are exercising the creative and technical muscles in your brain, and a lot of abstract work is really based on muscle memory. That's why it's important to get into the habit of regular painting.

On days you absolutely can't make it to your studio or creative space to create, spend some time in that space meditating, cleaning, organizing, reading art books, or whatever you can do to stimulate your brain.

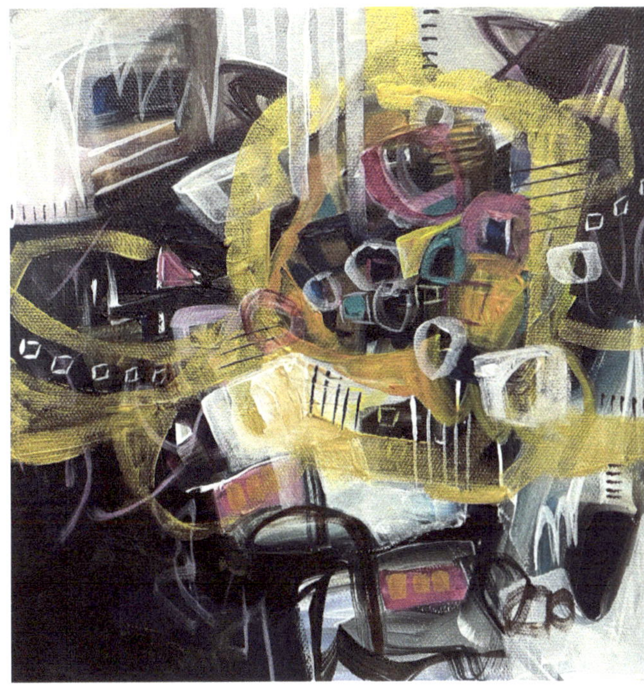

Thinking Out Loud
10x10 acrylic on canvas

Comparing Current Work to Previous Work

Every few months or every year, revisit some of your older work and see how far you've come. This is better than comparing yourself to other artists because it's not fair to you or them. You might love their work, but they might have started their craft way before you. Not only that, I do think artists develop at different rates. Some artists pick things up faster than others, and there's nothing wrong with that. There's no wrong way to make progress in art, as it's an individualized journey in which each person's path is unique.

Setting SMART Goals

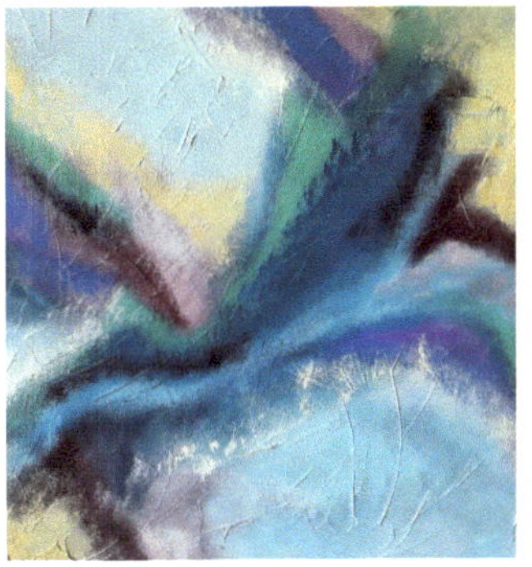

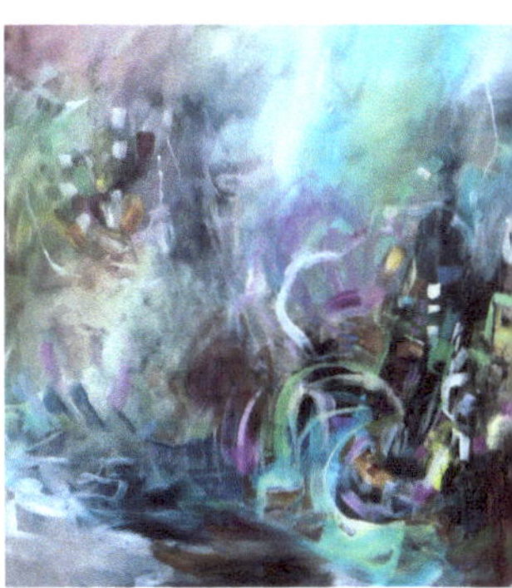

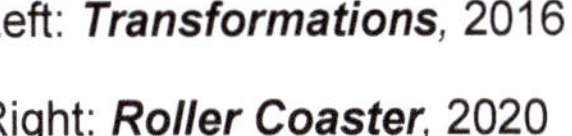

Left: ***Transformations,*** 2016

Right: ***Roller Coaster,*** 2020

SMART stands for specific, measurable, attainable, realistic, and time-oriented. For example, a SMART goal would not be "to paint more," but instead "to create 100 paintings by the end of the year." I'm a firm believer in setting SMART goals, because those are the only ones you can truly measure. More sample goals could include:

- Participate in three art festivals by the end of the year.
- Create a website to showcase my work by the end of the month.

- Attain representation with at least one gallery by the end of the year.

Finding Several Supporters

Find supporters of your work to give you honest feedback. Hopefully these individuals will be ones who can be honest about where you can improve, and what you are doing that is going well. For me, my family and several friends serve as my close supporters.

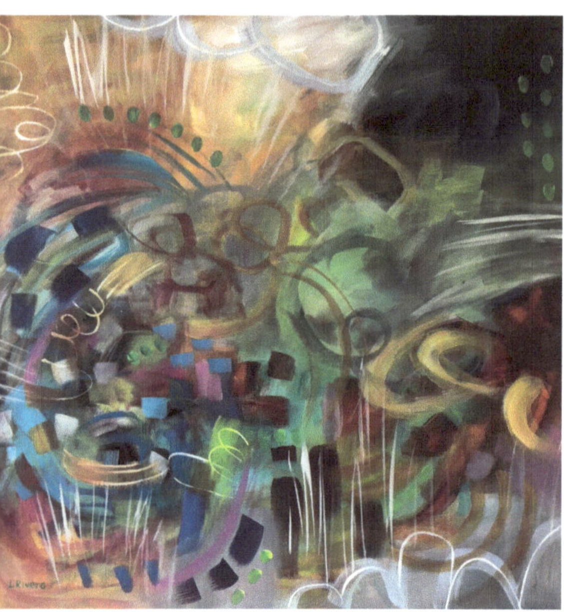

Sunshine on a Cloudy Day
24x24 acrylic on canvas

Taking a Class

Don't be afraid to take a class, any kind of class. It could be drawing, painting, ceramics, or anything you want more help with or want to learn. I believe that any kind of formalized art training will help you along the way. Even if you're a professional artist, there are always things you can learn from other artists. I really had to step outside of my comfort zone to take classes as I had never really painted in front of anyone. At first it was really uncomfortable, but the more I did it, the easier it became.

Paint 100 paintings in 100 days.

Painting 100 Paintings in 100 Days.

I started a project in 2019 of painting 100 paintings in 100 days. They were small abstract studies on 8"x8" watercolor paper. Doing that project taught me a great deal. You get better at painting the more you practice, just like anything else. I was trying to be playful and loose with these pieces and worked on paper, which allowed me more freedom to experiment. I experimented with composition a lot in the small paintings. You might have heard other people say if you want to get good at painting, set a goal to paint 100 pieces. I also highly recommend you do that. Put a time limit on the goal as well so you can measure it.

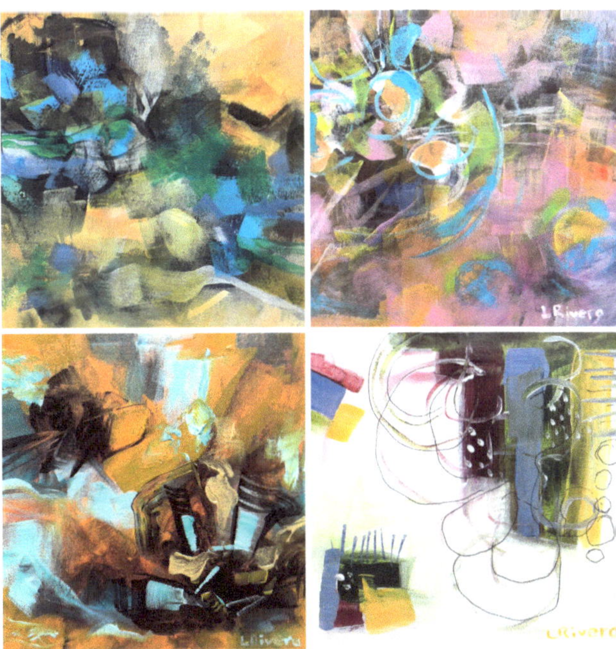

Paintings from 100 day challenge

Societal Views

I don't think I could possibly write an abstract painting book without mentioning where it stands among the general public. I know I mentioned this earlier, but I think it's worth another mention. It doesn't take an expert to notice that abstract art doesn't seem to be as popular as representational and realistic art. Many abstract artists' roots are actually in representational art and many also have well developed skills in drawing and painting objects.

Despite all of this, I want to encourage you to paint your passion, because your best work will shine through when you're painting what you want to be painting. If abstract art is your passion, paint abstracts. Don't worry about how well they are liked. You'll excel the most when you are painting what you want to paint.

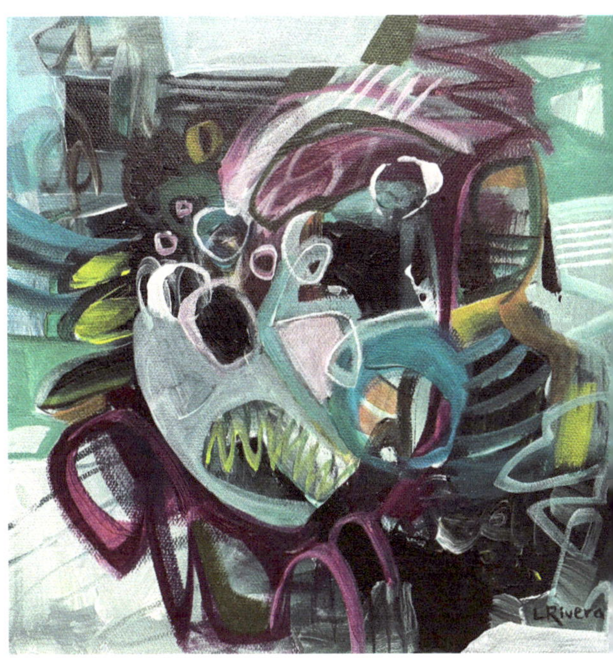

Emerald Fusion
10x10 acrylic on canvas

Connection

I think people have a need to feel connected to an art piece, and sometimes it's easier for them to make an emotional connection to recognizable objects or figures than textures, shapes, colors, and so on.

I also think people connect with abstract art by connecting with the artist. Maybe a collector has something in common with the artist, and that is what draws her in. If the artist aligns in any way with the viewer, it seems there is more of a connection to the artwork.

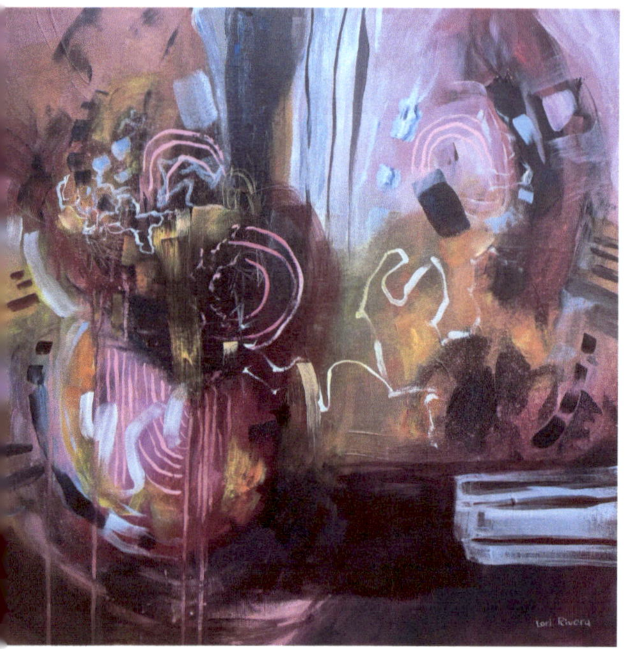

Embers
24x24 acrylic on canvas

Degree of Difficulty

It took me at least two solid years of painting to get to a point where I felt my abstracts were sell-able. I find creating abstracts harder to paint than most representational pieces. When I first started creating abstracts, I was happy with some of my pieces. As time has gone by though, I realize they were not very strong pieces, mainly in the composition. I've found that creating a good composition in an abstract piece is probably the most difficult aspect of working abstractly.

Once I started intentionally trying to create a good composition, I started to get better at it. I'm still learning, but of course, that will be the case for the rest of my life. Just like other artists, I'm a lifelong learner.

Abstract Art + Poetry

I look at abstract art as being very similar to poetry. Some poetry is the abstract art of literature and it seems to have a very niche following, just as abstract art does. Abstract art does have a following though, and you must attract that market if your objective is to sell your work.

Five + Alive
10x10 acrylic on canvas

Interpreting Abstract Art

Sometimes the wonder of abstract art is simply getting lost in the colors and the feelings the work evokes, without any external influence, or a title that tells the viewer what she should see in the piece. I love giving my paintings obscure titles so that the viewer is left to define the piece subjectively. I do occasionally give my abstract art objective titles, but recently I've been trying to stick with non-literal titles.

Abstract art truly has a language all its own, with each piece telling a unique story for each person that looks at it. I think it's amazing how a piece of art can be interpreted so many different ways from person to person, and that is one of the reasons I love abstract art. Each person connects to it in an individualized way. One of my favorite things to do is ask for interpretative feedback on my paintings, such as answers to questions like: 1) How does the painting make you feel, and 2) What does the piece communicate to you?

Let's see this in action. I posted the photo to the right to Facebook, and I'm sharing some of the responses I got.

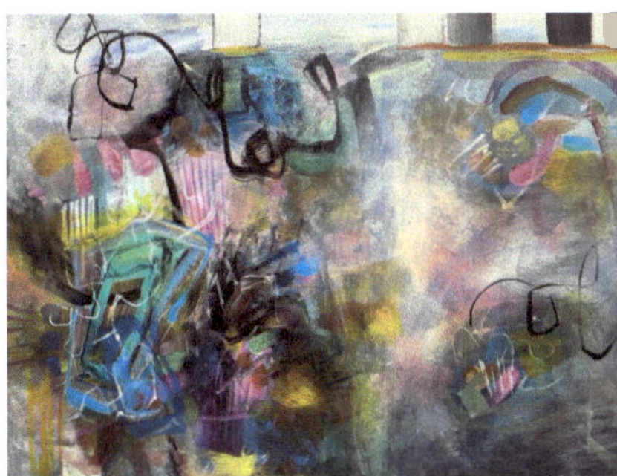

Late Night Convo
9x12 acrylic on watercolor paper

Option 1

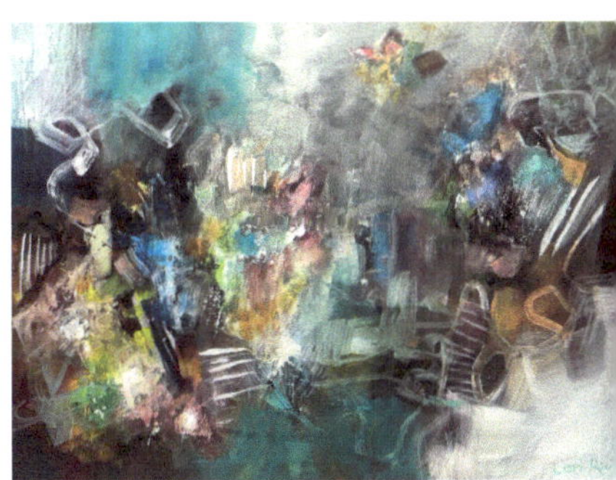

Burning the Midnight Oil
9x12 acrylic on watercolor paper

Option 2

Facebook post responses when asked if they prefer art piece #1 or #2:

"The colors in the first one seem unevenly distributed to the point that the left half is almost a contrast to the right half."

"I like how it looks like one side is talking and the other is listening in number one."

"Number two has more depth."

"What drew me into the first one was the black squiggle line up at the top like a phone cord and I enjoy the bubble gum pink areas on the first as well."

As you can see, the responses varied. It's very interesting asking for feedback on my paintings because I never know what kind of responses I'm going to get. I love the response that stated, "it looks like one side is talking and the other is listening." And then when

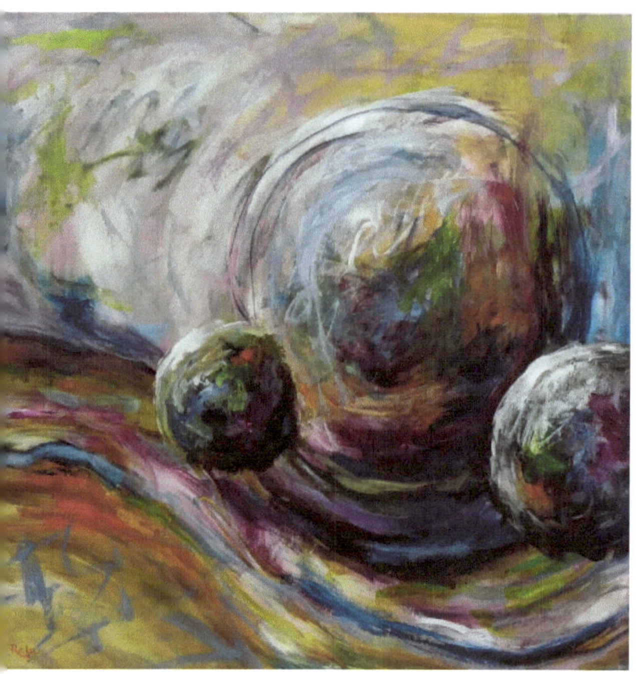

Playing for Keeps
20x20 acrylic on canvas

another person thought the black squiggle reminded her of a phone cord, I thought I chose the perfect title because I actually painted this piece while talking to a friend.

Sometimes it's fun to hear what kind of objects people see in an intended nonobjective abstract piece. But other times, you'd rather not hear, because once they mention what they see, it seems that's *all* you see.

My husband and daughter are always telling me what they see in my paintings. Most of the time it's okay, but my husband once told me that he saw boxing gloves in my painting "Playing for Keeps." Now I just can't "unsee" them. Ultimately, I want the viewer to enjoy the exploratory and experiential nature of viewing abstract art subjectively.

Exercises

Defining Your Abstract Style

Do a Google search for abstract art, and ask yourself: What do I like and not like about the pieces I'm looking at?

Create a Painting Schedule

It's so important to maintain a regular painting schedule, so I encourage you to take a few minutes and plan out when you will paint each day. I paint while my daughter is in school and I work at the frame shop on Wednesdays and Saturdays. My goal is to get roughly three hours of painting in each day, or 21 hours a week. When I can fit it in, I paint on the days I work at the shop as well.

The exercise on the previous page will help you define your abstract personality. Do you like tightly painted work, or do you like work that's loosely done? Are you drawn to bright and bold colors or more neutral palettes? These are just a couple of questions that the exercise will help you answer, and this will provide some general direction for you. But ultimately, I encourage you to work intuitively and driven by emotion, but also influenced by the external environment, which brings me to my next point.

Do you like tightly painted work, or do you like work that's loosely done? Are you drawn to bright and bold colors or more subdued palettes?

Art lies on an internal/external continuum with internally driven on one end and externally driven on the other end. An example of an internally driven piece would be a nonrepresentational abstract based on emotion, and on the externally driven end would be a hyper realistic objective piece of artwork.

This continuum is somewhat hypothetical, as I don't really think art is ever entirely internally driven or entirely externally driven. I think even the most abstract painting has some external influence -- whether we are influenced by the music we are listening to, a conversation we had with a friend yesterday, or travel memories from years ago. The same goes for externally focused work, which can reflect the internal personality of the artist through the chosen subject.

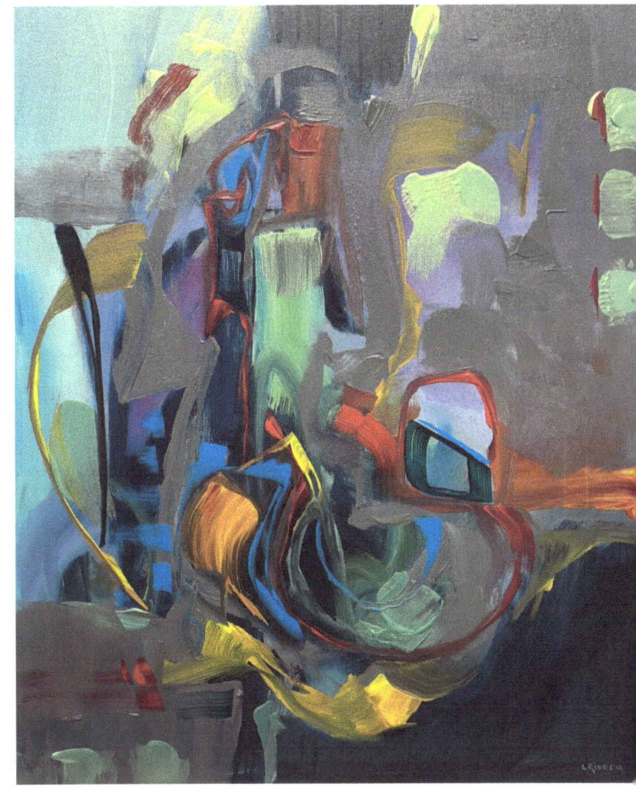

The Lucky One
24x20 acrylic on canvas

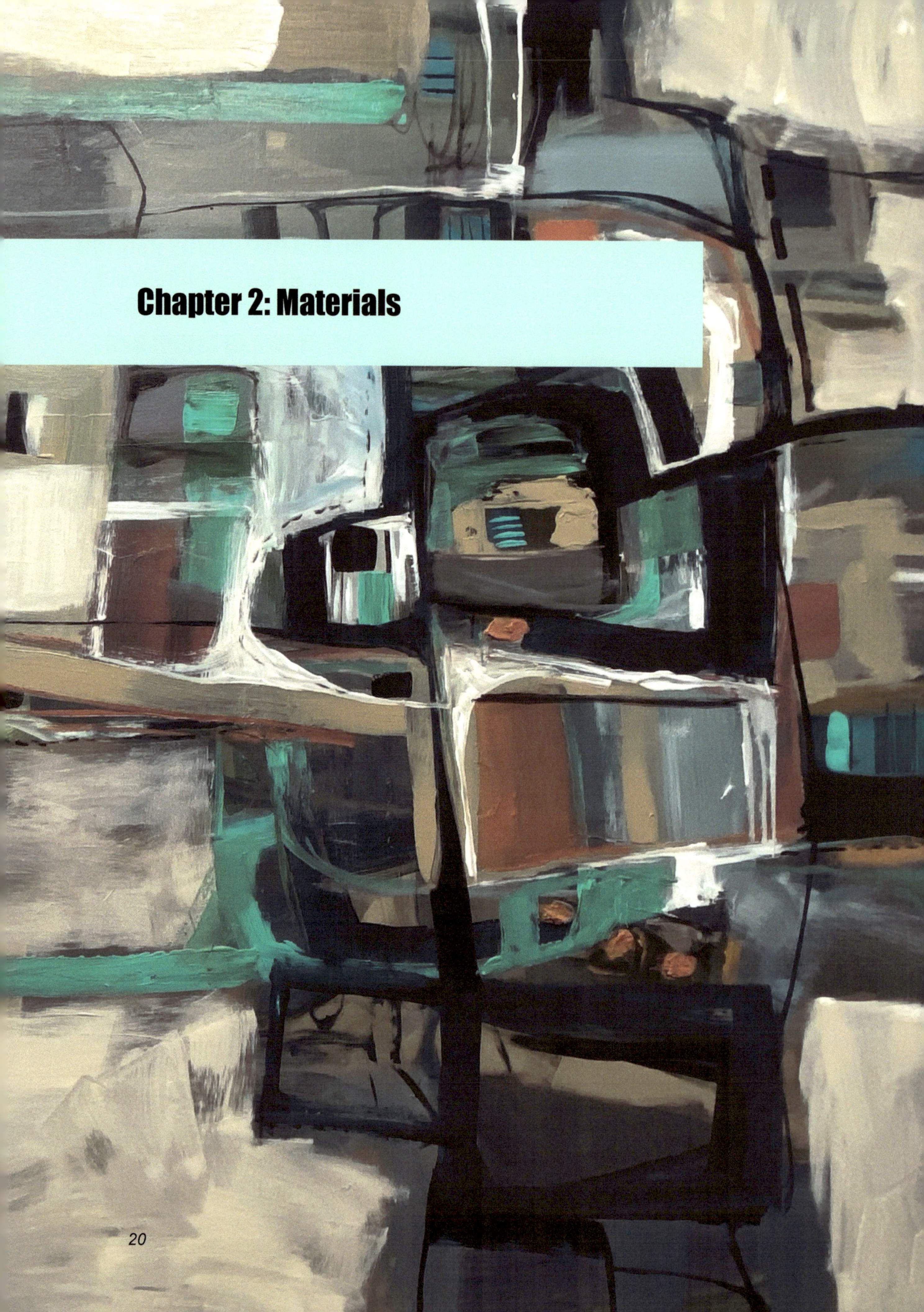

Chapter 2: Materials

Materials

When you're first starting out, you don't need to purchase professional grade paints, but I do recommend getting the best quality paints you can afford. While higher quality materials won't make you a better painter, these materials will make the painting process easier. For example, better quality paints are more pigmented. You'll find that with lower quality paints, you need to apply more layers than you do with higher quality paints to achieve the same look.

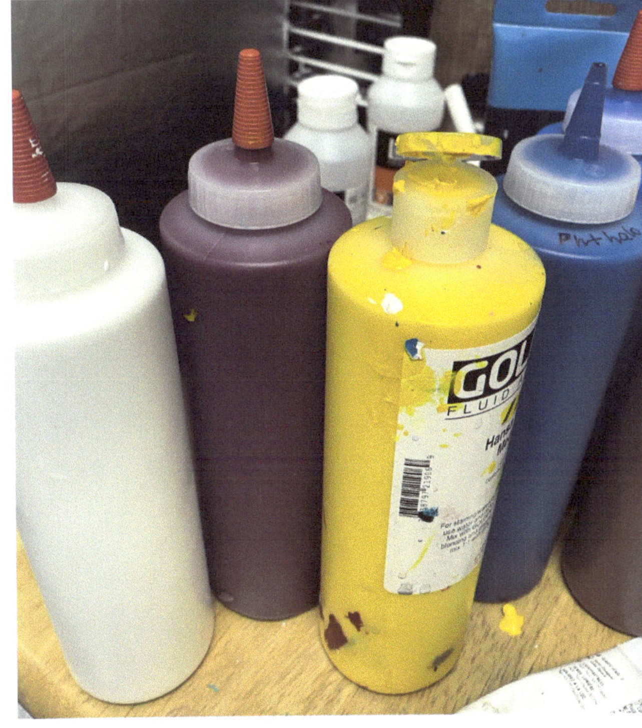

Acrylic paints

I think you are fine buying cheaper materials for certain things, such as brushes and palette knives. While you don't want brushes that are going to shed bristles in your paint, I've purchased multi-pack brushes at art stores and they worked great. Also, I think the white plastic palette knives work fine. I don't think it's necessary to get expensive ones.

I also use lots of foam brushes when I paint abstracts. I usually buy them 50 at a time on Amazon. Foam brushes work great for painting abstracts, especially when you're covering a large area. Oftentimes, I even use the same foam brush for a couple different colors without even washing out the brush in between. Eventually the foam brush gets too muddy, though, and I have to get a new one or wash the current one out.

As far as your surface (substrate), I recommend starting out using canvas panels or canvas paper for your paintings. You can get these for a fraction of the cost of canvas and wood. And you'll feel much more free to experiment if you are working with inexpensive materials. Sometimes, using large, good quality canvas can feel very confining due to the fear of ruining the canvas. But you can always go back and paint over the canvas with gesso and start a new painting on top of it. You don't even have to really go over it with gesso. If I paint over a finished painting, I just add paint right on top of the painting without a layer of gesso first. Sometimes it's nice to let some of the underneath layers peek through the new layers.

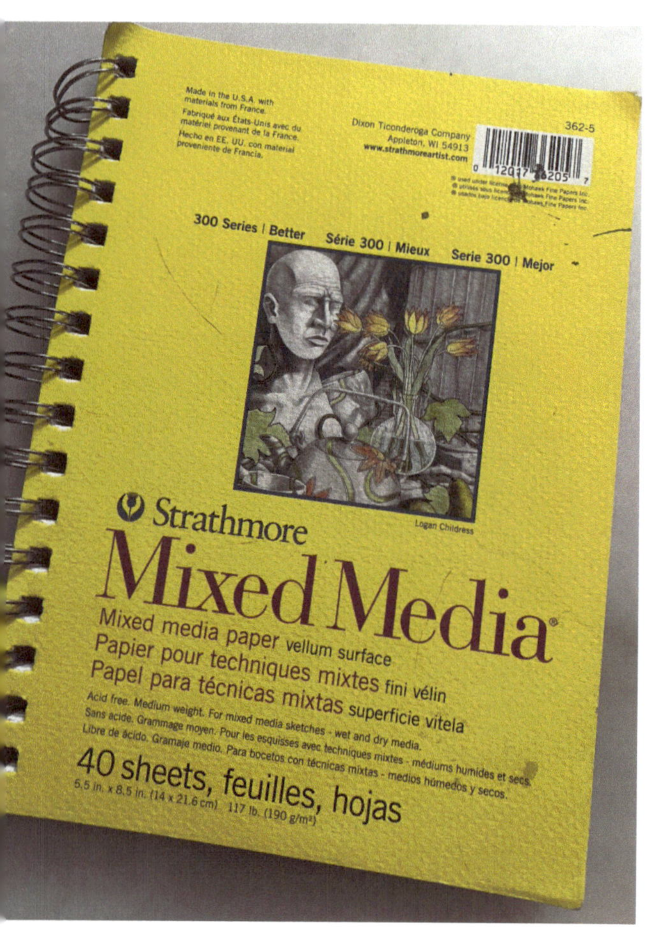

Mixed media paper

You can also paint on mixed media or watercolor paper, but I'm not a big fan of painting on paper. Even if you add a few coats of gesso first, the paint soaks in to the paper so quickly. But I encourage you to try it out for yourself and see if you like it. You may find you love working on paper.

Also, these paintings you create in the beginning can serve as jumping off points for larger pieces. I recommend starting out with abstract studies around 9x12. As soon as you get comfortable with that size, move up to 16x20, and so on. Every time you get comfortable with a certain size, then size up, and keep doing this until you are painting sizes you aspire to create. The largest painting I've ever created is a 48x60, mostly because I can't accommodate larger than that size in my studio.

I do believe you will feel much more free using canvas panels, watercolor or mixed media paper at first. Many artists don't like canvas panels as some don't consider them archival. I was painting on canvas panels quite a bit for a while, simply because they are so economical. A fairly inexpensive alternative to canvas panels that I have found are the gessobord panels. I get mine from Jerry's Artarama or Blick Art Materials and I love painting on them. I like how sturdy they are and they can be framed easily. Another thing I like about them is that you can be rough with them and add lots of texture, including crackle paste. Some texture mediums like crackle paste don't work well on pliable substrates like canvas. I find the gessobord panels work better for my abstract landscapes than my nonobjective abstracts though. I encourage you to try all the different surfaces to see what you like best.

Something you'll find over time with experimentation is that each substrate (panels, canvas, paper, wood, etc.) acts a little differently, which also changes the look of your pieces. You'll find what you like to use.

My favorite paper is Fluid brand watercolor blocks and I like the cold pressed option because it has a little texture. There is also hot pressed watercolor paper that has a very smooth surface. One thing to remember is that certain surfaces, including paper, you'll have to put a couple layers of gesso on first before painting because the paint is soaked up fast without it. Even with the gesso, paintings on paper dry pretty quickly. You must work really fast if you're trying to blend. Another paper I've recently discovered that I love is the Strathmore mixed media 400 series paper.

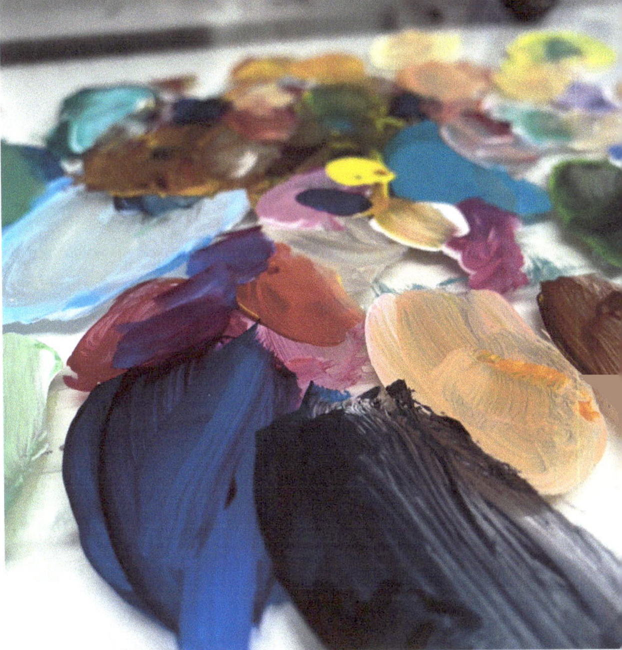

My tabletop glass palette

Paint

I use acrylic paints because they work so well for abstracts, and I really just prefer them because they dry fast. I've tried using oils in abstract work, but have just not been as pleased with the results. That's not to say you can't use oils for abstracts, because you certainly can, and many do. My personal preference is acrylic, though, and the way I work in layers really lends itself well to acrylics.

I definitely don't recommend buying one of the starter paint sets.They usually include colors you really don't need, and don't include ones you do need. It might take some trial and error, and a lot of paintings for you to define your color palette, but keep with it until you find a color palette combo you love and can't live without. I talk more about color in Chapter Four.

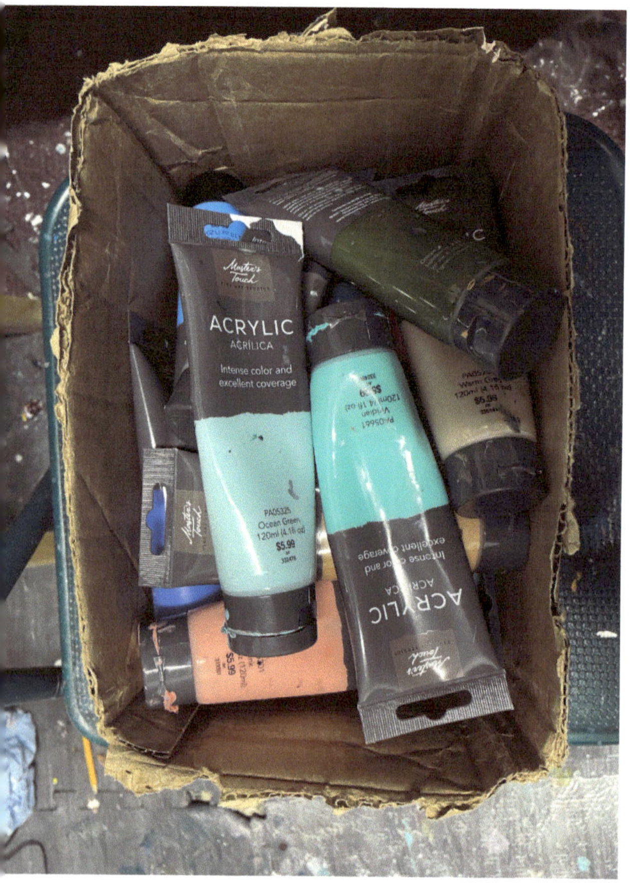

Many times I start out my paintings using five out-of-the-tube colors from Nova Color, which I mix to make unique colors. If you choose, you can use a limited palette. I used a limited palette for my abstracts for about three years. I talk more about limited palettes in Chapter Four. Just recently I've started using more inexpensive and thicker paints for the texture in my paintings. I like the Master's Touch brand at Hobby Lobby for my texturing paints and buy them when they're 40% off. Just today I got a haul of twelve tubes of paint for under $50!

Master's Touch paints

If you're looking for good quality, inexpensive paints that you can apply very thickly without feeling like you're breaking the bank, I recommend Master's Touch or Liquitex Basics.

You can use everything from craft-grade acrylic paint to top-of-the-line acrylic paints in your abstracts. You'll find that better-quality paints provide a more enjoyable painting experience because they're usually more pigmented. I use a wide range of paints, including Blick brand, Liquitex Basics, Liquitex heavy body, Golden, Grumbacher, Winsor & Newton, and several years ago I started using Nova Color paints.

Using a limited palette of five colors will help you learn how to mix colors. You can use white, a yellow, a red, a blue, and a brown like burnt sienna. From these few colors you can mix a wide range of colors, and all your secondary colors (oranges, greens, and violets) can be mixed from them.

Recently I decided to place all my "limited palette" Nova Color paints into squeeze bottles. I'm finding I waste a lot less paint by doing this because I can control the amount that comes out of the bottle. Nova Color brand paints are very pigmented, but thin enough that you can pour them from a squeeze bottle. Over time, you'll get a feel for what viscosity paints you prefer - thin or thick paint, and a lot of it will depend what kind of look you're trying to achieve in your paintings.

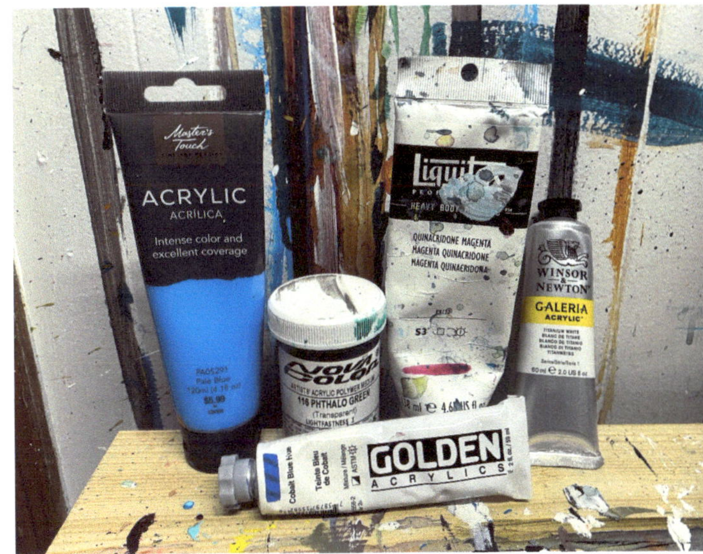

Various brands of paints

Can I mix different brands of acrylic paint?

All the choices in an art store can be so overwhelming and can leave you with more questions than when you first went in. Should I paint on paper, canvas, or wood? What kind of easel is the best? Then you walk down the paint section, and not only are the colors endless, but it also seems the brands are endless, which is why I always stress using a limited palette and mixing your colors. You can add additional colors to your limited palette as desired or needed.

In general, you can mix any brand of acrylic paint with other brands of acrylic paint. There are heavy bodied acrylics, fluid acrylics, high flow acrylics, and others, and you can mix all of them regardless of brand, color, or viscosity. One exception is that you might not want to mix "open acrylics" (which dry much slower) with other acrylics, because the open acrylics might lose their properties. Just know, too, that if you mix two different paints with different viscosities, the thickness of your mixed color will be different.

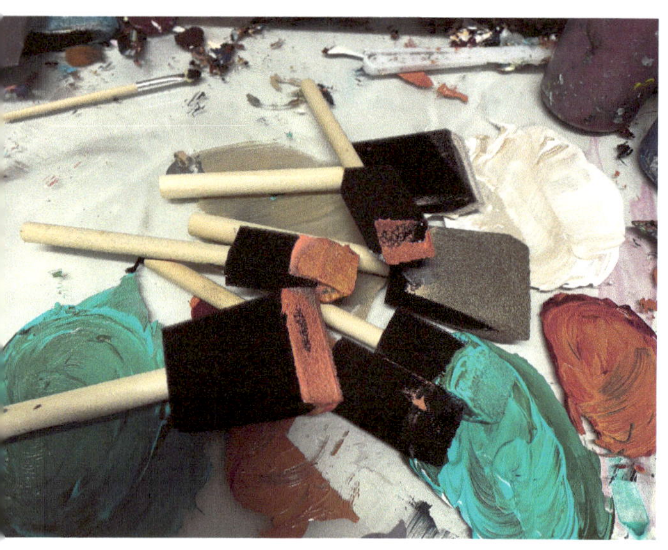

Foam brushes + acrylic paint

When you work with colors outside your limited palette, it also gets trickier to match colors later, unless you make a note of the colors you used. I have started writing the names of the colors I use in each of my paintings in my database to make this easier.

The most important thing to mention here is that the same colors in different brands are not created equal. For example, turquoise in one brand might be brighter than another brand of turquoise. Just be mindful that when you mix the same color in different brands, you might get varied results. Despite this, you can still mix different brands and colors.

Substrate (the surface to which you are applying paint)

For this book, my examples are on both canvas and paper. When I work on paper (even though it's not my favorite), I use Fluid watercolor blocks of paper because there is binding at the top and the bottom, and this binding helps to prevent the paper from warping as you're painting. I paint on the paper while it's still attached to the block. An alternative is taping your paper down to a drawing board. I suggest if you paint on paper, get at least 140 pound weight or higher. The higher the better.

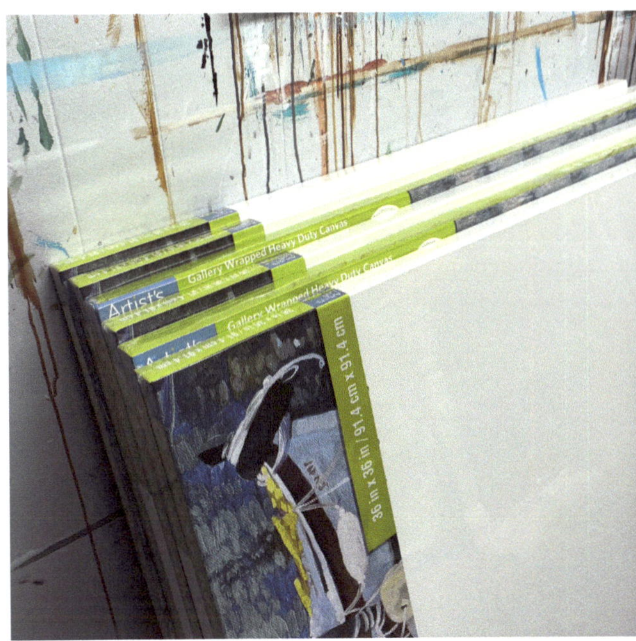

36x36 canvases

You can really paint on nearly anything with acrylics. The surfaces I mentioned above are probably the most common. Just add 2-3 coats of gesso on almost any surface you paint on with acrylics. Most canvas panels and canvas already come with gesso applied, but paper and wood usually don't.

Palettes

Paper painting palettes are nice because you can throw them away when you're done painting. You can also use paper plates or almost any flat surface you don't mind getting paint on. I try to set up my palette the same way every time. It makes painting more efficient when there's no guessing where your colors are.

Recently I've been attaching parchment paper to a TV tray with tape and using that as a palette. I'm finding it works quite well. After I'm finished with the palette I just pull the parchment paper off the table and throw it away. Then the next time I paint, I put new paper down.

A smooth glass cutting board works great as a painting palette and that is what I use sometimes for smaller pieces. After you paint you can remove the paint by spraying it with water, and then scraping it off with a glass scraper. You can even use a large sheet of glass and set it on your table to use as a palette. I also use this method. A large piece of glass covers three quarters of my painting table.

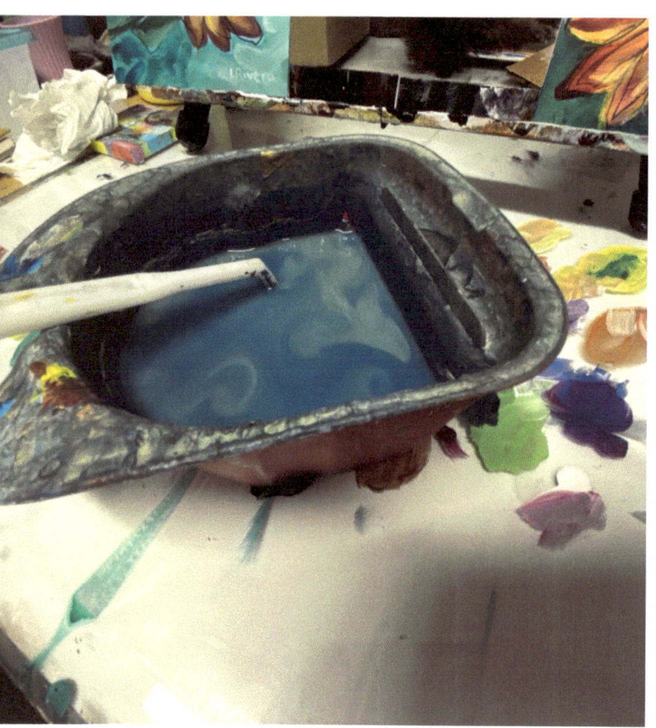

Water

Water + Water Container

Acrylics are water-based media, and most people do add water to their acrylic paints, but you don't have to. It really just depends on what kind of look you're trying to achieve.

The bigger the painting is, the bigger water container you might need. Or you might just have to change your water often if you have a small container. When using acrylics, you'll need the water for rinsing out your brushes, and to add water to your brush before dipping it in the paint, unless you're going for lots of texture! Then you'll probably apply the paint without water.

When painting abstracts, I rarely use water, except to rinse out my brushes. I find that it's easier to create textured paintings without water because the water thins down the paint too much.

Paper Towels and/or Old Cloths

Use paper towels or old cloths to dry off your brush after rinsing it in water. I like using the blue shop towels because they're thicker which means they last longer. I purchase them from Amazon by the box. You can also use paper towels to remove some of the paint from your brush before washing it out. This will prevent you from having to change your water as often.

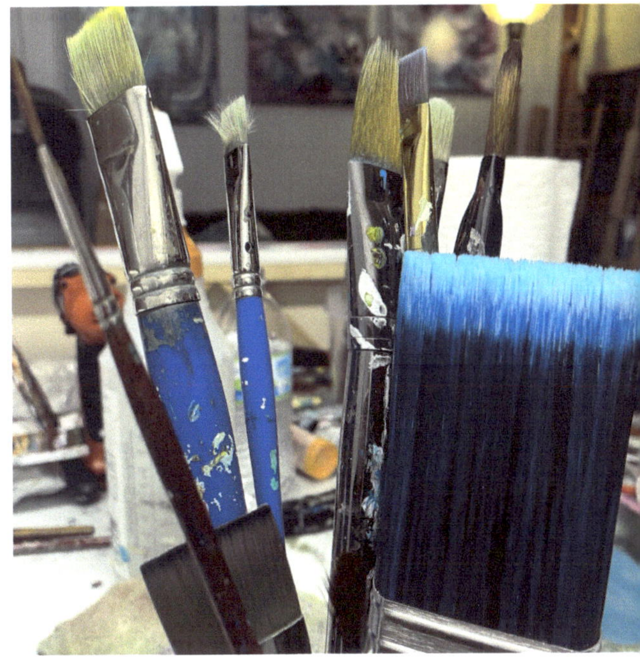

Paintbrushes

Paintbrushes

Paintbrushes come in many brands and a range of prices and sizes. The variety brush packs at art stores are fine to use. The main drawback of some variety packs is that they are usually short handled. I love long handled brushes since they help me paint in a looser style.

I used to spend a lot of money on brushes until I tried a variety pack and loved them. I don't have a problem with the bristles coming out like I thought I would. Sometimes the bristles of cheap brushes fall out and get in your painting. My favorite brushes that are also affordable are the Blick brand student brushes (blue handle).

I also find that 2 and 3 inch foam brushes are great to use and cover large areas at a time. I use mostly foam brushes when painting abstracts, except for fine details.

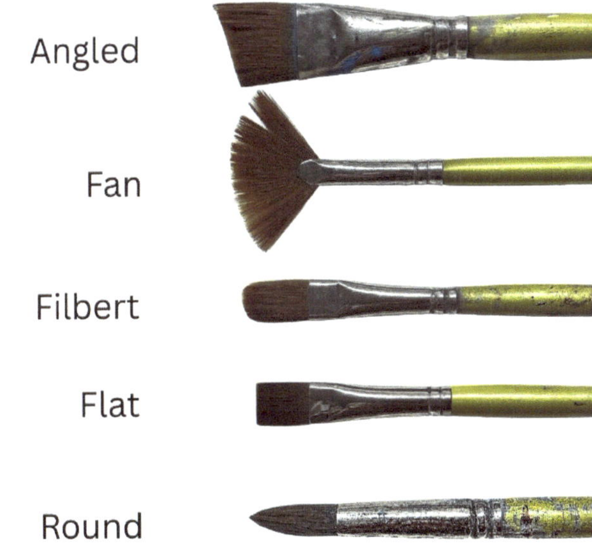

Shown above are several types of paintbrushes.

Gesso

Before you paint on any surface with acrylic paints, it is highly recommended that you apply 2-3 coats of gesso as a primer (unless your surface is pre-gessoed). When working on paper and wood, this helps the paint from

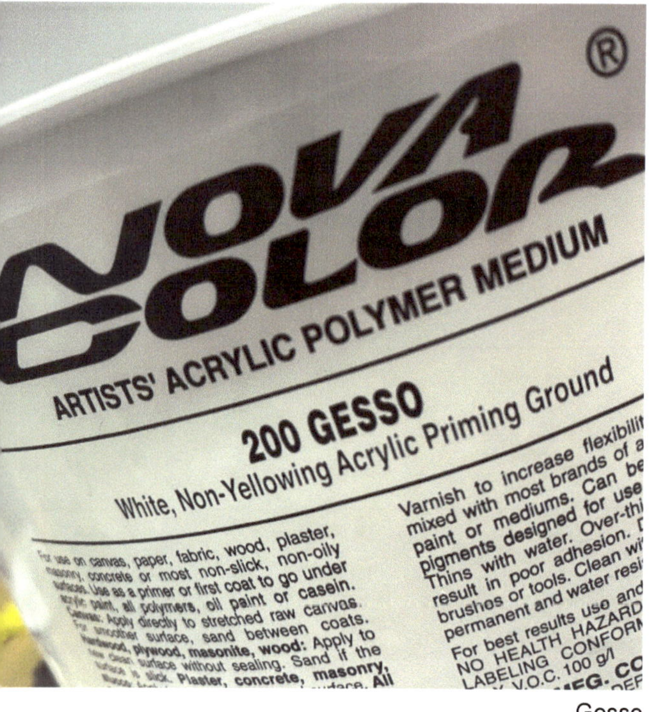

Gesso

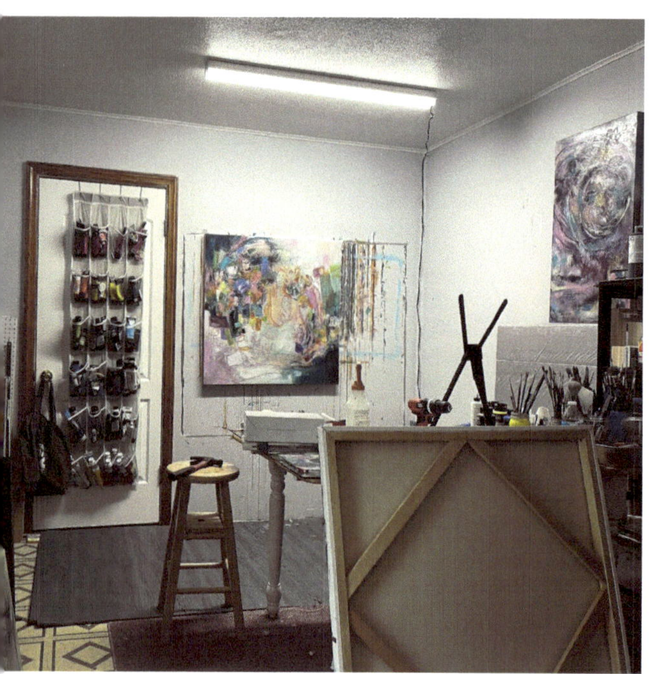
My painting wall

absorbing so quickly. You can expect coats of gesso to dry within about 10-20 minutes, depending on how thickly you apply it. Canvases and canvas panels usually always have gesso on them already, so you shouldn't need to apply coats of gesso to those.

You can also purchase unprimed rolled canvas, and in that case, you would want to prime the canvas with gesso before painting on it. If you've ever tried painting on unprimed canvas, you know that the paint absorbs quickly, which results in needing much more paint than if the surface was primed first.

Easel

Some painters prefer to paint on a table and some prefer to paint on an easel. You'll find what works best for you. For smaller pieces, I use a tabletop metal easel that I got on sale for just $10. If you're painting large scale, you'll want a floor easel, or you can hammer in two nails the same height on the wall and hang your pieces right on the wall to paint them. Painting with my canvas straight on the wall is my favorite way to paint larger canvases.

Varnish

Something I used to not be able to live without is varnish. After your painting is totally dry (let dry for about a week), you can apply a varnish for protection and to add an even sheen. Sometimes when you use different brands of paint, each will have a different sheen, but varnish can give your painting a unified look. Varnishes come in matte, satin, and glossy.

My favorite varnish is Nova Color matte (dries as satin) Also, make sure to get all the photos you need before varnishing, especially if you're using glossy varnish. The glossy varnish will reflect light and make it difficult to photograph. Don't forget to sign your piece before you add the varnish as well.

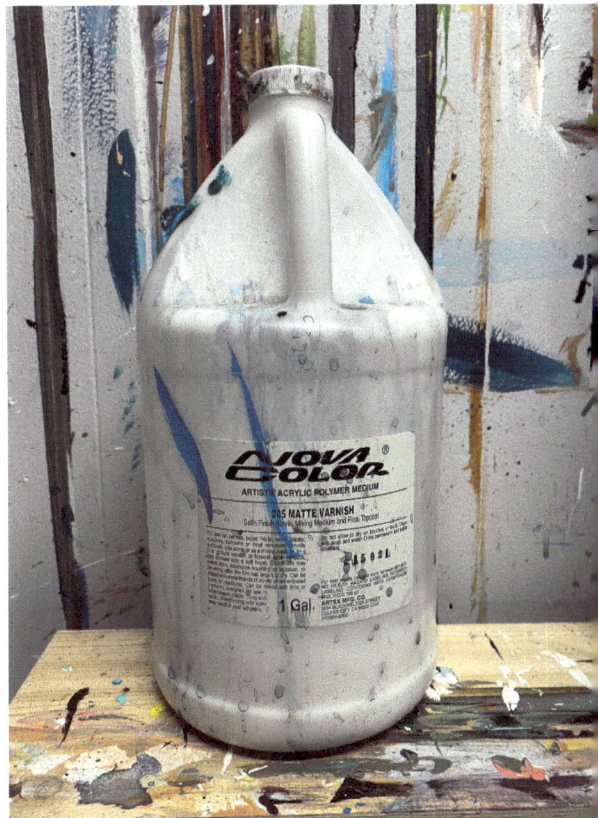

Nova Color varnish

With all that being said, I no longer varnish my paintings. I stopped varnishing them a couple years ago after I read in an article that if varnish is removed from a painting, it can actually damage the piece because the varnish is made of the same materials as the paints. I just really find it an unnecessary step, unless you're wanting a shiny finish. Unless someone places a painting in direct sunlight, varnishing really isn't needed. I'm sure many painters would disagree with me, but that's my opinion. I encourage you to do your own research online about varnishing and then decide if you want to varnish your paintings. I think it's really just personal preference.

Acrylic Glazing Liquid

Acrylic glazing liquid is my favorite acrylic painting medium. You can add semi-transparent glazes on your work with glazing liquid, and I often use it to quiet down areas of the painting so they're less busy. I like having a mixture of busy and quiet areas in my paintings. The quiet areas allow the eye to rest while the busy areas energize the viewer. You can mix glazing liquid with any acrylic paint to add a glaze. I use Nova Color varnish as my glazing liquid, which is more economical than purchasing actual glazing liquid.

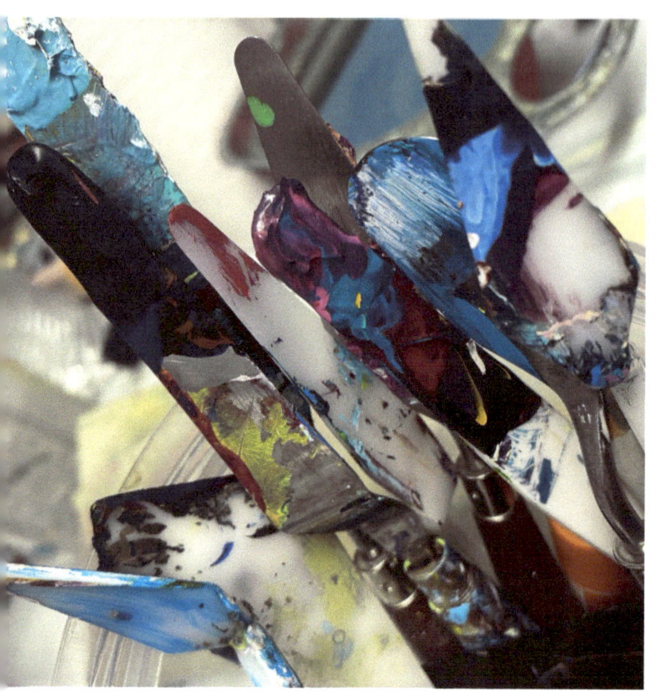

Palette knives

Palette Knives

Palette knives are great to have, whether you're painting your entire piece with palette knives or just using them to apply thicker areas of paint. I often use palette knives to place thicker areas of paint, and then mix my colors on the surface. You can often achieve a looser look with palette knives as well.

Other Materials

There are tons of other materials you can use in your work. When more than one medium is used, your piece is then referred to as "mixed media" instead of an acrylic painting.

Some other materials include: pencil, ink, charcoal, paper, chalk pastels, oil pastels, and mixed media crayons. There are many others that I haven't listed! Experiment with these other materials as your heart desires. In this chapter, I have just talked about what I use most of the time. Most of my paintings are just that - acrylic paintings. I mostly just use acrylic paint in my abstracts, but I would love to start exploring the incorporation of other media into my work.

Something important to note here is that you can use oil on top of acrylic, but not acrylic over oil. If you decide you want to experiment with oils, including oil pastels, just remember that they will have to be applied on top of the acrylic!

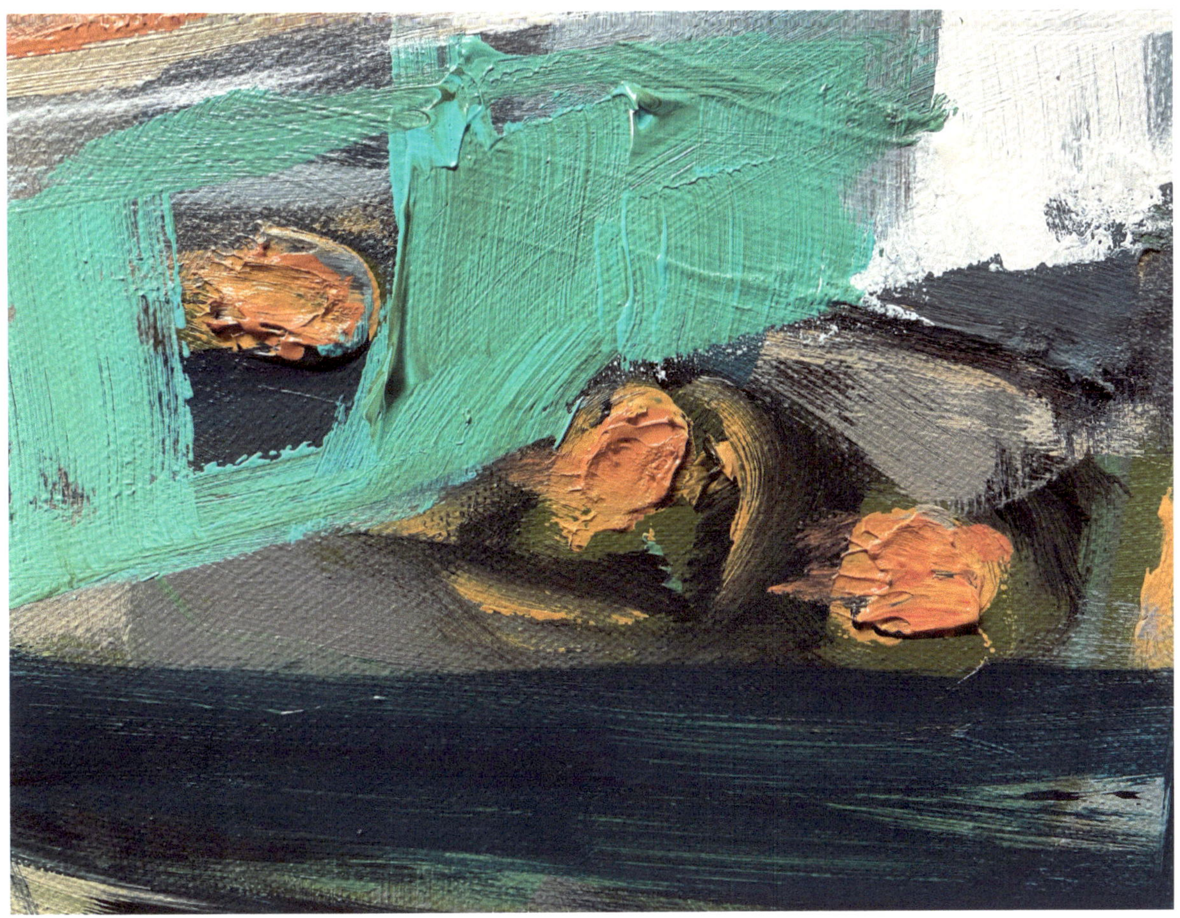

Paint applied without water

TIP: You don't have to paint with water. Acrylics can be used with no water added. You might try using no water if you are wanting an impasto (thick paint) look or if you are painting with a palette knife.

You'll find if you're using a brush, the paint glides easier with a little water. Without water, you get a thicker, more dry brush look, which is fine too. It is all about preference. I try to vary the types of brush marks in my work to add interest.

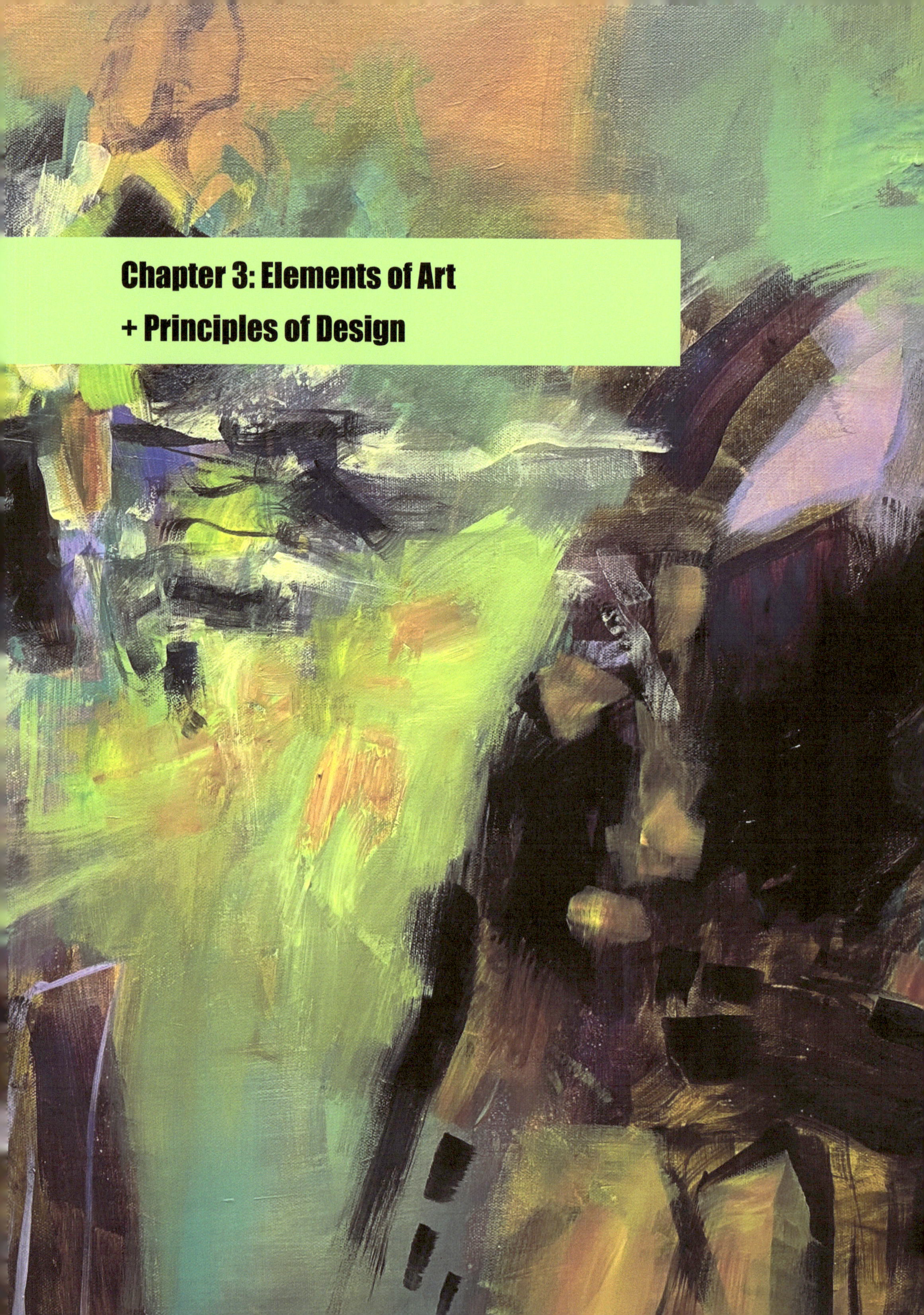

Chapter 3: Elements of Art + Principles of Design

Elements of Art + Principles of Dcsign

Artwork can't be created without the elements of art, and the principles of design helps you add visual interest to your pieces. Every artwork is made up of at least one element of art, usually more than one. Some artwork uses every element of art.

The elements of art and the principles of design are critically important in nonobjective abstract painting. In abstract painting, these are what really hold the painting together and allow it to stand on its own. With objective realistic painting, the first things I notice are the objects themselves and the emphasis seems to be on those objects. But in nonobjective abstract painting in which objects aren't being painted, the elements and principles become the stars of the pieces, which I think is why it's important to be familiar with them.

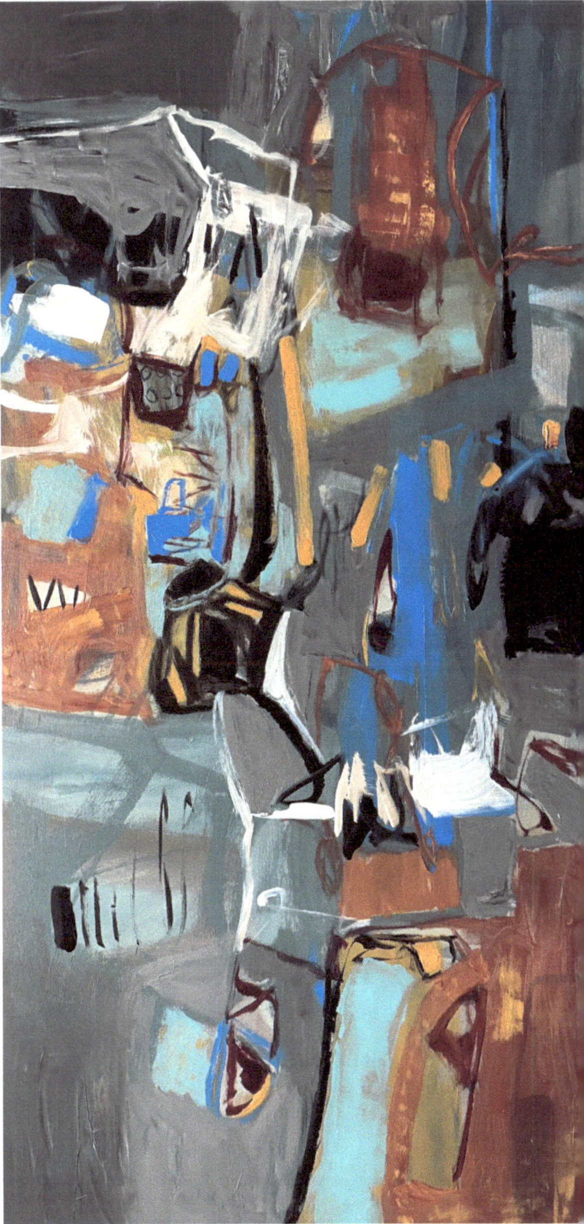

Into the Sun
48x24 acrylic on canvas

Elements of Art

You can find the elements of art in clothing, wallpaper, architecture, gift wrap, furniture, journals, notebooks, and many other everyday objects. As you know, art is everywhere; we just have to open our eyes and minds to be sure to notice it.

How you use the elements of art depends a lot on your style. Maybe you paint shapes rigidly, or maybe you prefer organic and loose shapes. Are you drawn to 2D or 3D effects in your paintings? Do you use bright colors or more subdued colors? All of this deals with the elements and how you use them in your work.

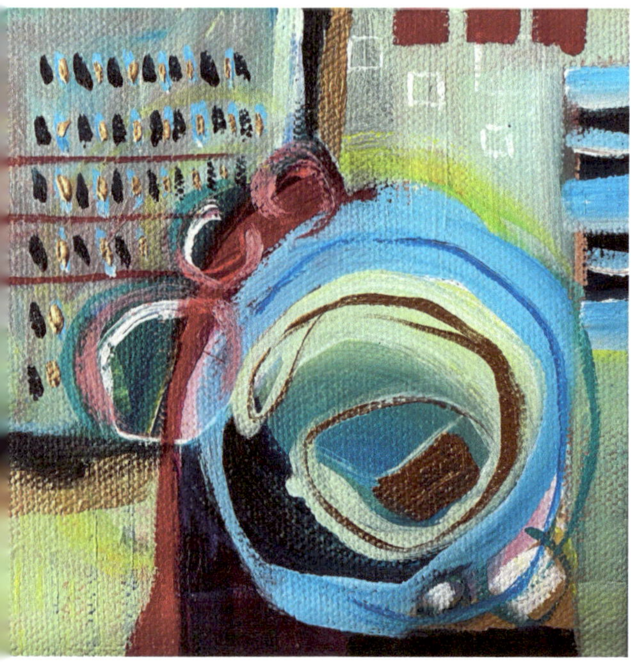

When the Sun Goes Down
4x4 acrylic on canvas

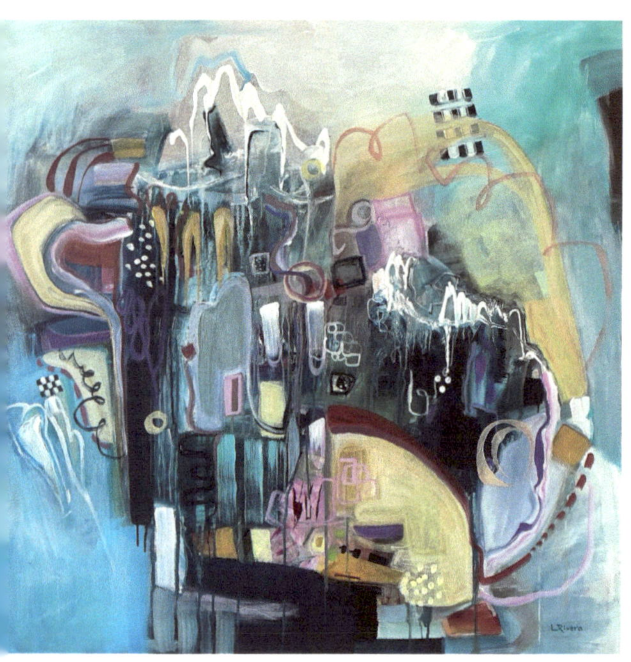

Big City Dreaming
36x36 acrylic on canvas

You can play with a couple of the elements or all of them in your paintings. Once you start painting more and more, the less thought you'll put into each painting. The elements will appear in your work organically and you'll start creating via intuition.

With the examples of my art that I give, you can see the interplay of multiple elements in each piece.

Color

Color has three properties, hue (name), intensity (also known as chroma, brightness, purity, or saturation), and value. The hue is simply the name of the color, the intensity is the level of brightness (see Chapter Four on Color for reducing the brightness). The value of the color is the lightness/darkness of it.

There's also the temperature of a color. Colors can be either warm or cool. Typically the warm colors are red, orange, and yellow, and the cool colors are green, blue, and violet. However, there can be warm colors and cool colors of every color. For example, there can be both warm reds and cool reds. Warm colors come forward in an artwork, and cool colors recede.

Sometimes I will add a certain color only to the focal point in the piece, as I did in "Pivotal," (right) to draw more attention to it.

I explain more about color in Chapter Four.

Shape

A shape is a two-dimensional area made of a line that intersects with itself (squares, circles, triangles, etc.). Shapes can be geometric or organic. Geometric shapes are rigid with defined lines. Organic shapes are loose and free, often found in nature, and free-flowing. "Free Rhythms" has a lot of geometric shapes in it.

Amazing examples of artworks that use shape are the works of Russian painter Wassily Kandinsky (1866-1944), who is considered the father of abstraction. His work also uses lines in masterful ways. Hilma Klint (1862-1944), who is believed to be the first abstract artist, even before Kandinsky, is another great artist to look up.

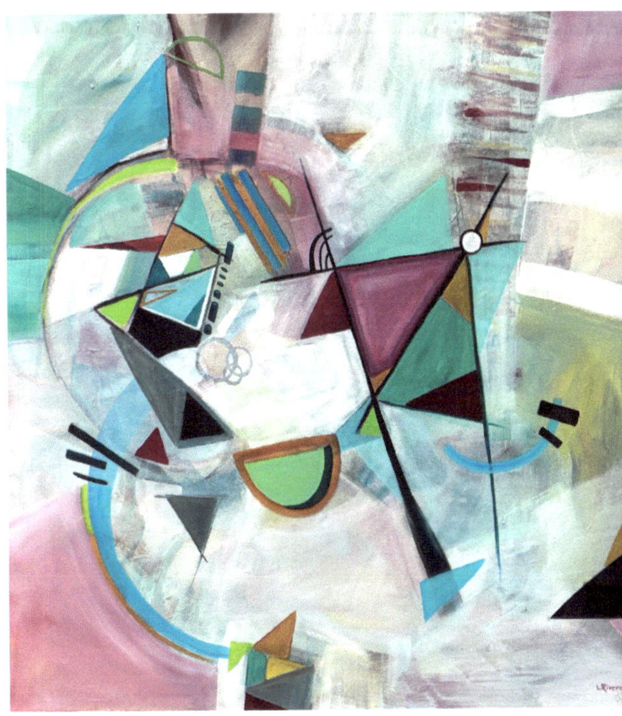

Free Rhythms
36x36 acrylic on canvas

Form

Form is any object that is 3-dimensional. A shape can take on a 3-dimensional qualities through the use of color and value. Three different values can create the illusion of a 3D shape, as shown in "Pivotal." Three-dimensional shapes have height, width, and depth and can be tactile or implied. Tactile forms would be things like pottery and sculptures. An example of an implied form would be the cubes in "Pivotal." The cubes in this painting are created using three different values. Cubes, cones, and spheres are all examples of form.

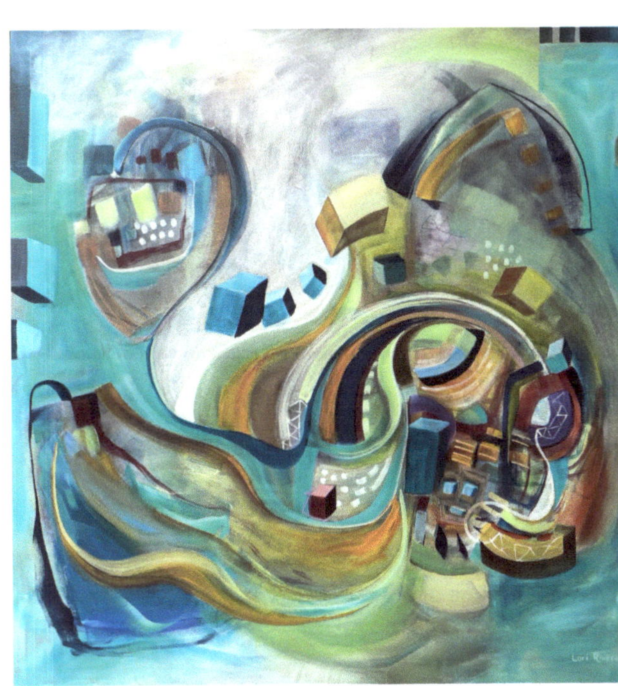

Pivotal
36x36 acrylic on canvas

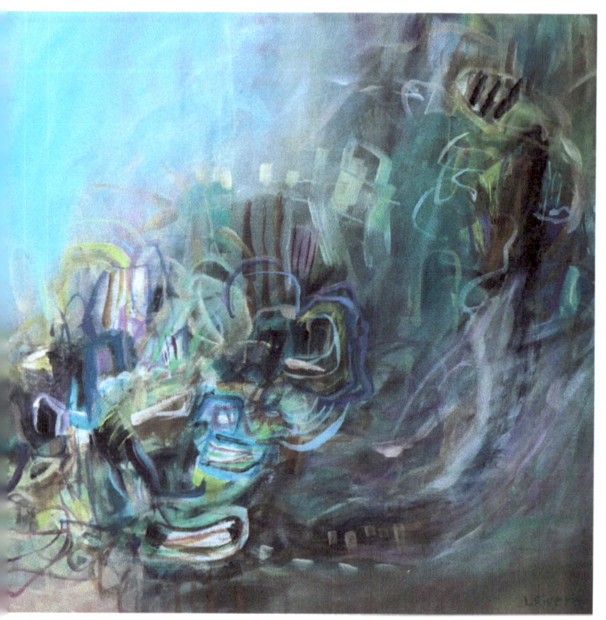

Wizardry
24x24 acrylic on canvas

Space

Space is in and around objects. Space can be positive or negative. Positive space is made up of the objects and negative space is the area between and around objects. "Wizardry" has a large area of negative space in the upper left.

The illusion of space can be created in many different ways. Artists can overlap objects, place objects higher to make them seem farther away, give objects farther away less detail, make objects farther away smaller, and make objects farther away cooler in temperature and lighter. Think of a landscape with mountains. The distant mountains are lighter, smaller, and have less detail than the mountains closest to us. These same techniques can be used in abstract painting and this is one way you can give your paintings more depth.

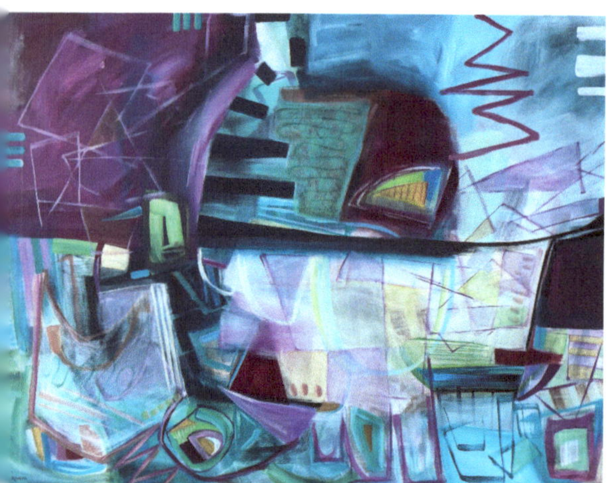

No Escape from Reality
36x48 acrylic on canvas

Line

Line is the mark made between two points. Lines can be painted in any direction, and can be straight, curved, zig-zagged, horizontal, vertical, diagonal, solid, dashed, dotted, thin, or thick. Lines can have a geometric feel (very straight) or an organic, loose feel. The lines in "No Escape from Reality" feel more geometric. Line can also be implied, such as the horizon line in a landscape.

You can use lines to direct viewers to the focal point in your painting. Vertical lines can depict strength and energy and can give a spiritual vibe, horizontal lines can communicate calmness, and diagonal lines can suggest motion. Zig-zag lines, like those in "No Escape from Reality," communicate energy.

Texturc

Texture refers to the look and feel of an artwork. In painting, the texture can even be implied. "Victorious has lots of implied texture, meaning the way I applied the paint gives the look of texture. But if you physically touched the painting, you wouldn't be able to feel anything because the texture is simply implied with the paint.

You can achieve real texture in your paintings by applying thick paint, using texture medium and gels, or by adding other media such as crumpled tissue paper.

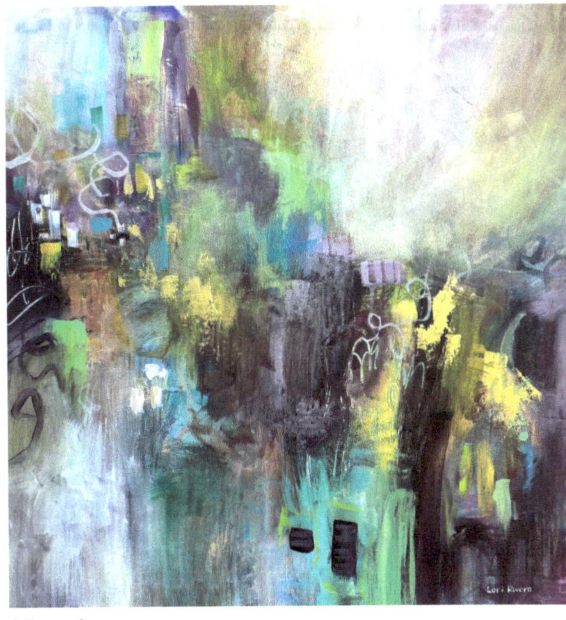

Victorious
24x24 acrylic on canvas

Value

Value is the degrees of lightness and darkness in a painting. You can paint some pieces in grayscale (white, black, and grays) or in monochrome (varying tints and shades of one color) to practice recognizing different values. You can get varying shades by adding black and tints by adding white. I like to mix a dark color (dark brown, dark blue, or dark purple) other than black, to make colors darker. When you mix pure black, it can make the mixed color lose its brightness.

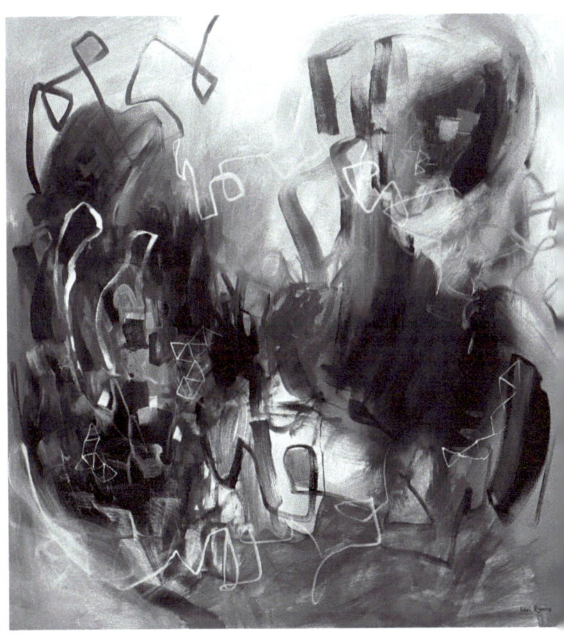

Gravity Pulling Violet

converted to black and white

Sometimes I use my phone to convert pictures of my pieces to grayscale to make sure I have enough value contrast. Over time you will get better at detecting values. In the grayscale format of "Gravity Pulling

Violet," you can easily see the values. Value can be tricky because some colors have the same value and will just appear as a big solid color when placed next to each other. Create as much value contrast as you possibly can in your paintings to add interest.

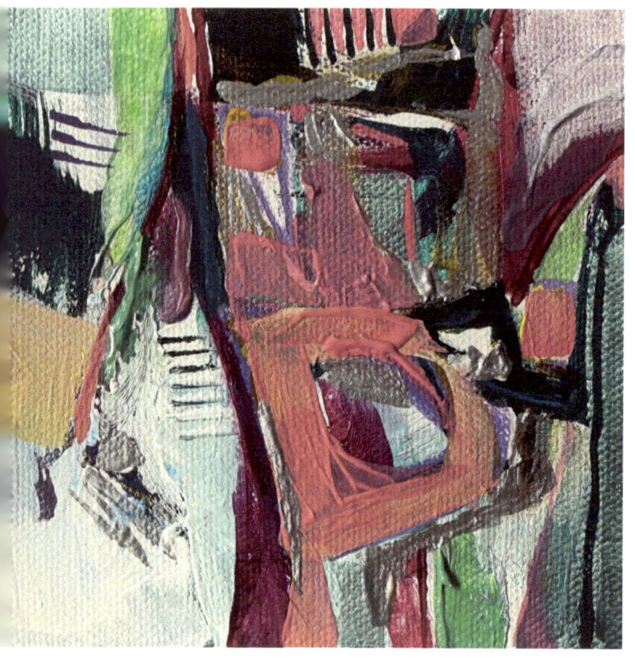

Forget What We're Told
4x4 acrylic on foam board

Paintings can be low-key, high-key, or use a wide range of values. Low-key paintings use dark values, and high-key paintings use light values.

Especially in representational painting, value is more important than intensity. For example, a portrait could be painted with many colors for the face, but if the values are correct, it will still look like a face.

Principles of Design

Balance

Balance is how the weight of elements is distributed around the piece. Symmetrical balance is when each side opposite from each other are the same. Asymmetrical balance is when the objects are different, such as having one large square on one side, and three smaller squares on the opposite side.

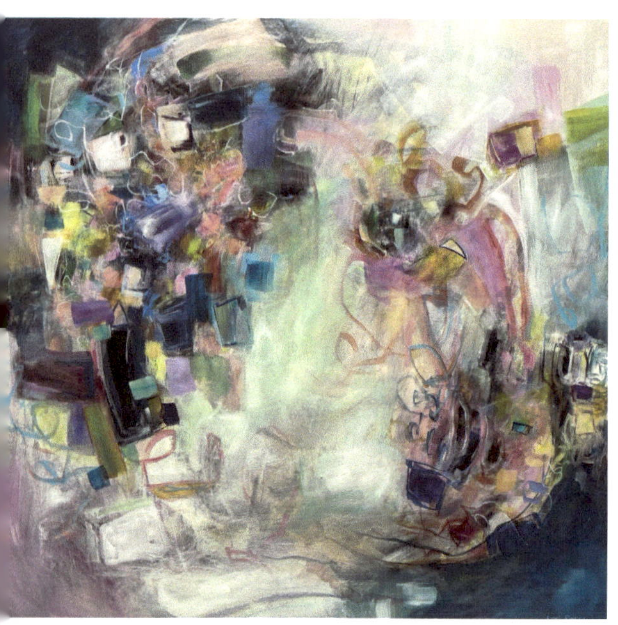

Becoming Centered
36x36 acrylic on canvas

You usually won't want opposite sides to match exactly because that creates a boring piece. But as you can see with "Becoming Centered," even though it's essentially balanced, each side is a bit different, with the left having more shapes and the right having a large solid area to the bottom right.

Once again, Kandinsky is a great example of an artist who was a master at using asymmetrical balance.

Unity

A piece has unity if it looks complete and harmonious. The best way I can describe this further is by asking the question -- does this piece look like three different pieces thrown together or does it look like one cohesive piece? One way to achieve unity is by using repetition, as I did in “You Can Go Your Own Way.” I repeated lines, shapes, and dots throughout the piece.

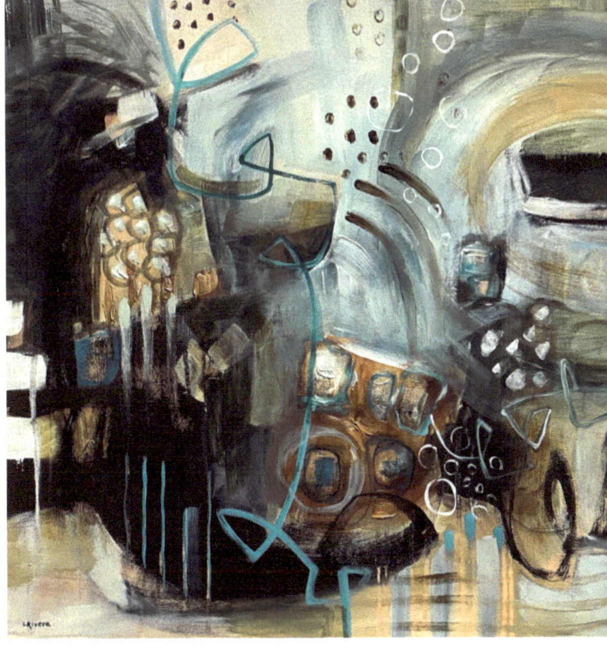

You Can Go Your Own Way
24x24 acrylic on canvas

Variety

When an artwork has good variety, it simply means that the artist has used elements in different ways, such as different colors, different shapes, different sizes, etc. Variety adds interest to your pieces and prevents them from being boring or monotonous. “Felicity” has different sizes of shapes, varied colors, and different lines to create interest.

The more variety you can add, the more interesting your artwork will probably be. However, you want to be careful and not make your piece too busy because it might become chaotic. It’s also good to have areas of rest in your painting. Notice how “Felicity” has some rest areas in it - both to the top and bottom left. The bottom right is less busy too, and I would consider that a rest area as well.

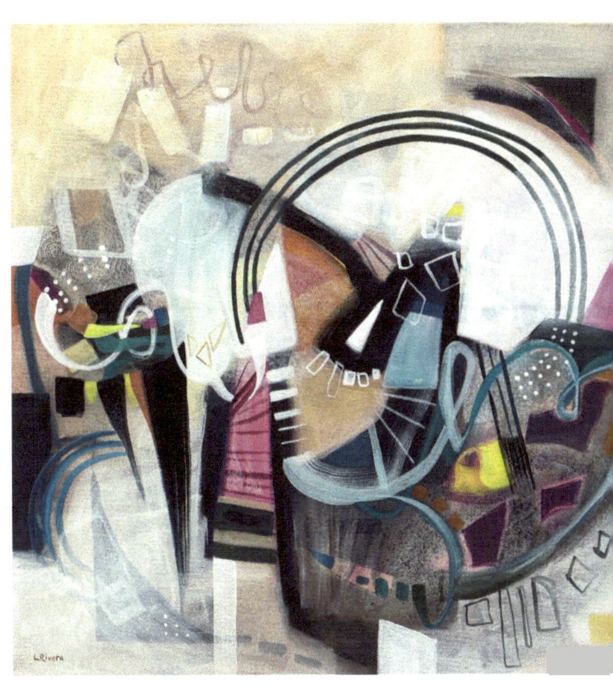

Felicity
24x24 acrylic on canvas

Emphasis

Emphasis is the part of the artwork that you notice first, and artists can define that emphasis through the use of elements. Usually you place emphasis in your focal point areas. In "Pink Punch," I've used almost a pure white and a pure black in the upper right-hand corner to create a lot of contrast. I would consider this the focal point of the piece.

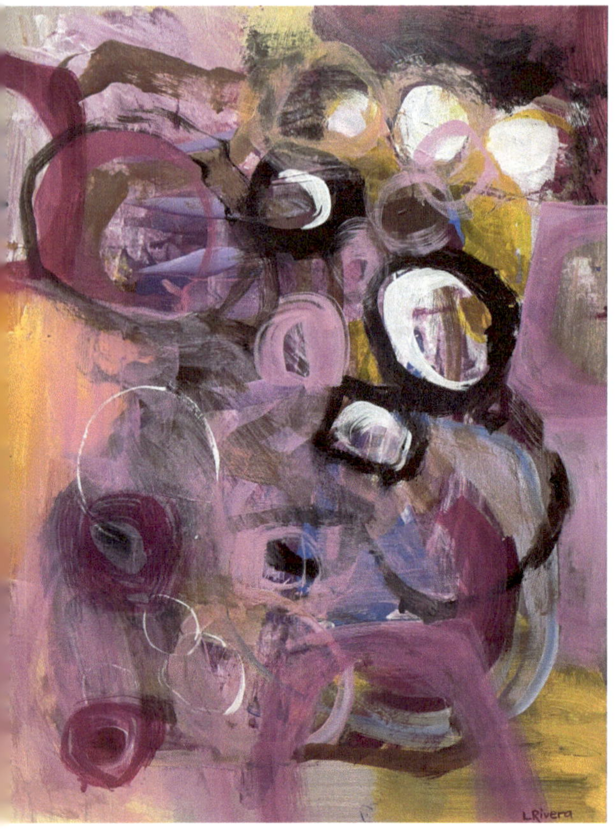

Pink Punch
14x11 acrylic on mixed media paper

You can have more than one focal point in a piece, too. Remember the rule of thirds that I will also talk about in Chapter Six. The rule of thirds is when you divide your work into equal thirds both horizontally and vertically. The intersection points are where your focal point(s) should ideally be. But like I've mentioned in other places in this book, you can break the rules. But you have to know what the rules are first before you can break them.

Movement

In "In the Blink of an Eye," I've created implied movement with the repeated black lines (thin ones on the left and thick ones on the right). The slightly diagonal directions of these along with repetition give a sense of movement.

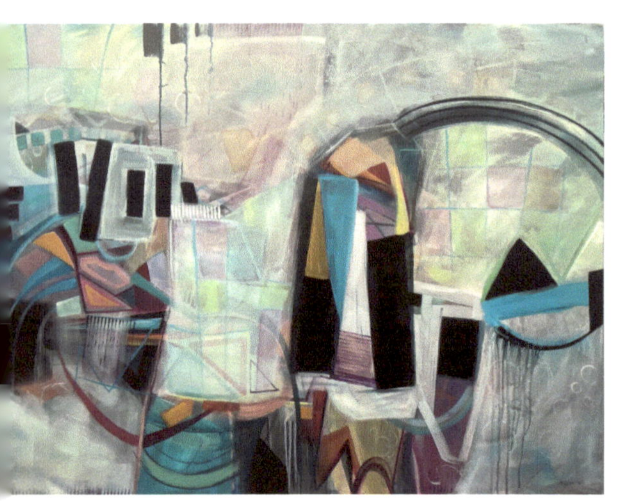

In the Blink of an Eye
36x48 acrylic on canvas

Repetition

Repeating elements keep a painting feel unified. Any of the elements of art can be repeated, including colors, shapes, patterns, and lines. See how I've repeated hatch marks, lines, and triangles in "And I'm Feeling Good?"

I think repetition helps tremendously in helping you create a cohesive work of art.

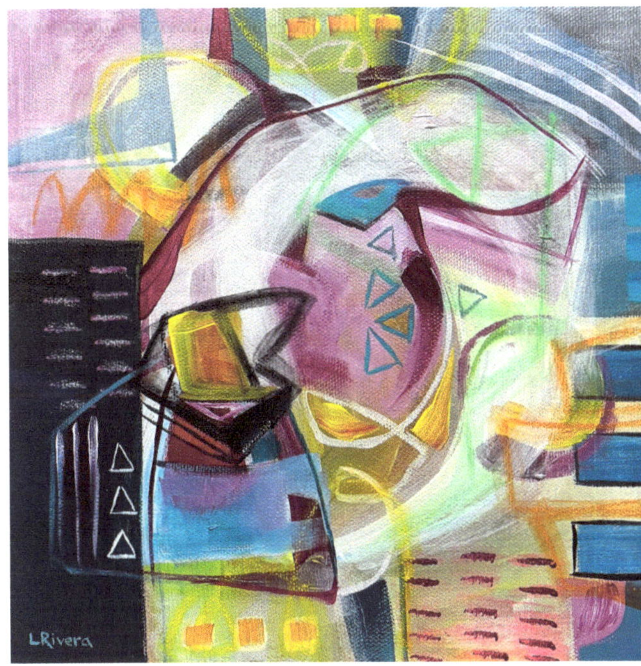

And I'm Feeling Good
10x10 acrylic on canvas

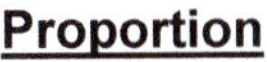

Proportion

Proportion refers to the size of the elements in relation to one another. It's good practice to vary the sizes of the elements in your piece to give it more visual interest. In "Intimate Conversation" I have different size circles, some open and some closed.

Proportion can also reference lines and whether they are thin or thick. You'll want both in your piece. With repetition, you usually repeat something exactly, but with proportion, you'll want to vary the sizes. Having both will make your painting interesting.

Remember also that smaller objects make them look farther away. This is how you can add depth to your painting.

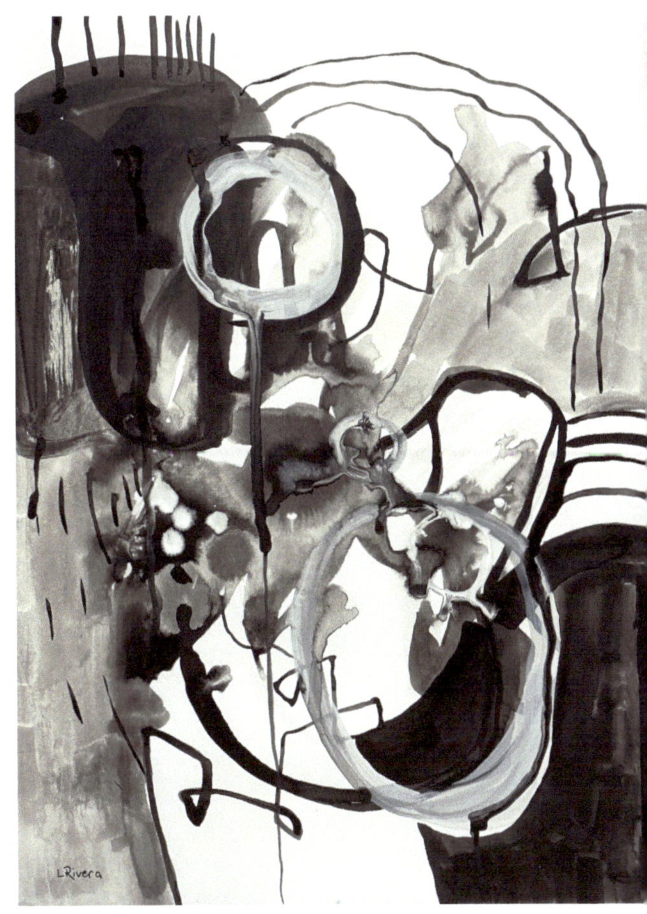

Intimate Conversation
12x9 ink on bristol paper

Exercises

Research Artists

Look up some famous abstract artists and abstract painters of today, and try to identify the elements in each painting you find. Instagram is a great way to find a wide variety of artists.

Demonstrate Your Understanding

Create paintings that demonstrate your understanding of each of the elements while also focusing on different principles of design; you may want to create many paintings to cover all of them. You'll find that each painting will most likely have several elements represented, if not all of them. Once finished with these, continue to use the elements and principles in all artworks you create.

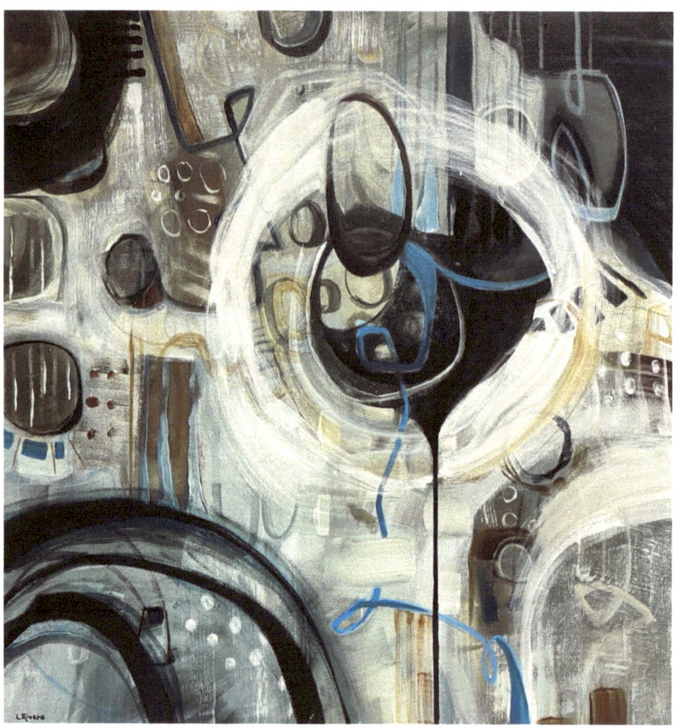

Onward
24x24 acrylic on canvas

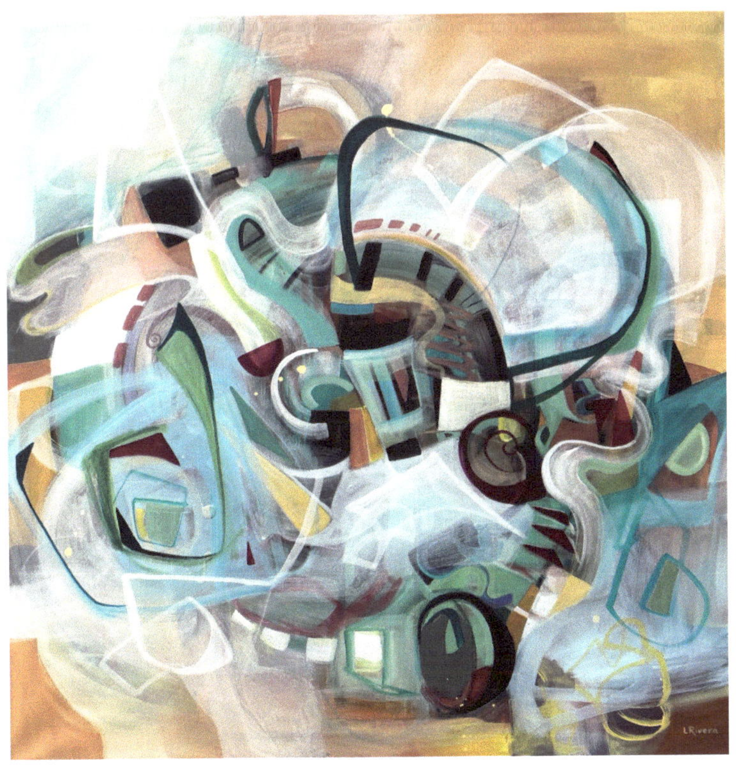

It Takes Two to Tango
36x36 acrylic on canvas

TIP: Working fast will help you paint in a looser style because it gives you less time to focus on fine details or "think" about what you are doing next. You can work faster by trying not to overthink your piece and simply by keeping that paintbrush moving. Try not to stop because each time you do, that gives you more time to think.

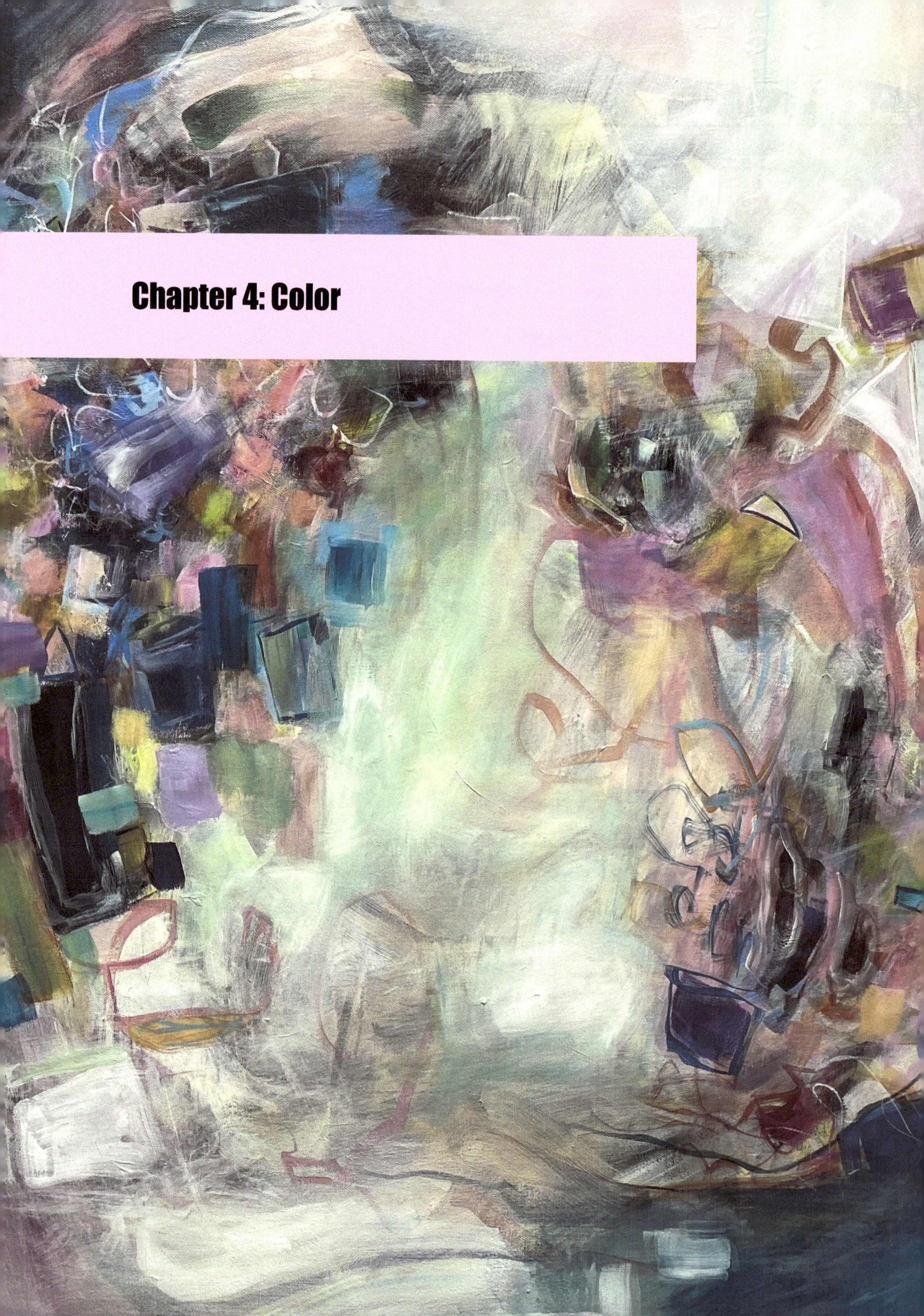

Chapter 4: Color

The Psychology of Color

In addition to everything I covered about color in the last chapter, colors can mean many things and can have different meanings based on context. You can take this into consideration, especially if you're wanting to give off a certain vibe. Following are some meanings associated with different colors.

Red
action, love, energy, strength, anger, excitement, danger

Orange
optimism, happiness, enthusiasm, vitality, creativity, excitement,

Yellow
warmth, hope, happiness, fun, joy, energetic

Green
nature, peace, health, new beginnings, money, growth

Blue
calmness, stability, sadness, trust, serenity, tranquility

Purple
royalty, uniqueness, creativity, mystery, luxury

Pink
compassion, femininity, softness, playfulness, romance

Black
formal, mystery, elegance, evil, darkness
sophistication, luxury, death

White
neutrality, hope, freshness, purity, innocence, elegance

Gray
calmness, conservative, balance, sophistication

Brown
warmth, honesty, earthy, natural

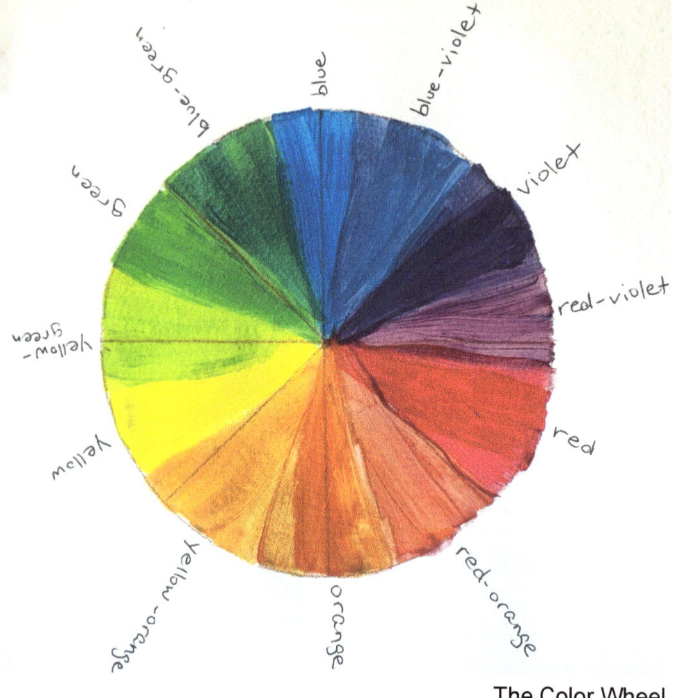

The Color Wheel

Color Wheel

There are many color schemes you can use. Complementary colors, which are ones opposite each other on the color wheel (red and green, blue and orange, violet and yellow) really pop in a painting. Analogous colors are next to each other on the color wheel (red, red-orange, & orange, or green, blue-green, & blue). There's also split complementary colors which is color paired with the two colors adjacent to its complement. An example would be red, yellow-green, and blue-green.

Get creative with your colors. There's an endless number of color combinations that look great together. You want your colors to sing, and choosing colors will become second nature the more you paint. You can purchase a color wheel at an art store. Having one on hand to look at will help you choose colors while you're painting.

Creating a Custom Limited Color Palette

Did you know using a limited palette is probably one of the easiest ways to brand your art and make it more cohesive? Have you ever noticed that you can recognize some artists' work just by paying attention to the colors they use? Chances are they always use the same color palette and mixing recipes. For several years, I used a limited color palette, which means I limited myself to only using a select number of out-of-the-tube colors. Even though it is called a limited palette, it doesn't mean you're more limited. Actually the opposite is true. Limited palettes force you to mix your colors so that your paintings will look more harmonious.

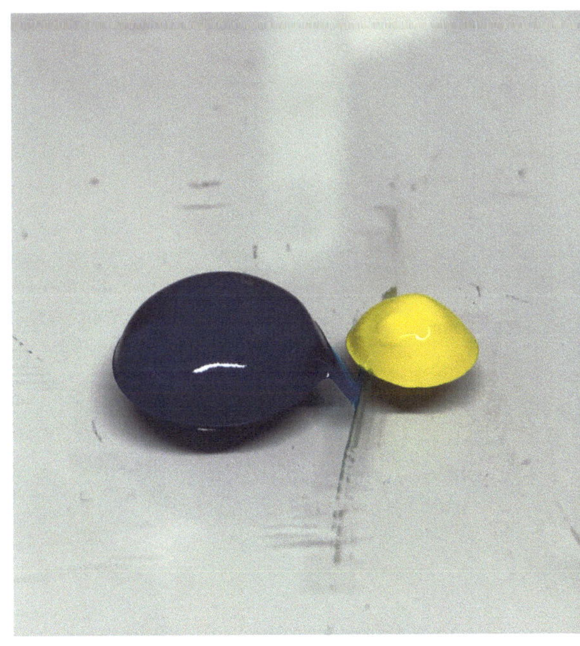

When mixed together, phthalo blue and cadmium yellow light make a beautiful dark turquoise!

Just recently I've started adding additional colors to my palette. I still start off each piece using a limited palette, then add additional colors as I go along, until I settle into a certain palette for each painting. Limited palettes are great for beginners, especially those who are learning how to mix colors.

When using a limited palette, I mix each one of my colors from the tube colors. I only use primary colors (red, yellow, blue) plus white and burnt sienna. I mix all of my secondary colors (orange, green, violet) from these. Probably about eighty percent of the time, I add another color with my colors out of the tube. I try not to use a color on my canvas straight out of the tube, with the exception of adding lots of texture towards the end of the piece. When I get to that point, I sometimes put paint directly on my brush from the tubes.

My limited palette colors are titanium white, cadmium

yellow light, quinacridone magenta, phthalo blue, and burnt sienna. I mix all of my greens, oranges, and violets from the primary colors, and I create black by mixing equal amounts of phthalo blue and burnt sienna. Recently, however, I've been experimenting with using straight black as it can add more moodiness. I create neutrals by mixing complementary colors, and adding white as needed to lighten. A wide range of colors can be mixed with these five tubes of paint. For those of you who may be new to using limited palettes, some basics are below. I substitute quinacridone magenta for red.

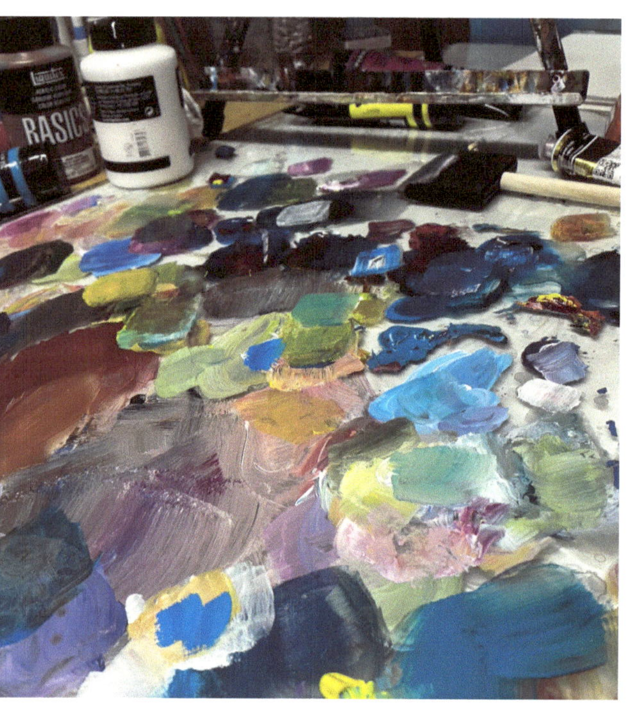

Paint palette

You may wonder why I am using magenta in my color palette instead of a truer red. Mixing a very small amount of cadmium yellow light to magenta turns it into a truer red, and I gravitate toward magenta (a cool color) more than I do to other reds anyway.

Primary Colors = red, yellow, blue

Secondary Colors = orange, green, violet

Tertiary Colors = red-orange, yellow-orange, blue-green, yellow-green, blue-violet, red-violet

Mixing Secondary Colors

Red + Yellow = Orange

Red + Blue = Violet

Yellow + Blue = Green

Add white to lighten (tints)
Add a dark color (dark blue, dark brown, or dark violet) to darken (shades). Try to stay away from using black to

darken your colors as this will decrease the brightness of the color. At the end of this chapter, I have you use black in a value exercise, but that's just for the purpose of the exercise.

To reduce the brightness of a color, add a small amount of its complementary color. I honestly don't use this technique often as I like brighter colors in my work, unless I'm adding neutrals. But if you like softer and more subdued colors, this technique will become your best friend.

Try to mix all of your colors and not use any straight out of the tube, or at least use sparingly.

Mixing complementary colors will give you wonderful browns and sometimes grays. Complementary colors are the best way to achieve unique and gorgeous neutrals.

Try to mix all of your colors and not use any straight out of the tube, or at least use sparingly. Mixed colors have a special quality to them -- mainly they don't look like they were squeezed out of a tube. Not only that, you don't want your colors to look like other artists' colors, who may be using the color right out of a tube. Mix when you can. Experiment with your colors to create a unique color palette all your own. There's nothing wrong with using paint right out of the tube, but you will find that many artists mix their colors and don't rely on manufactured ones.

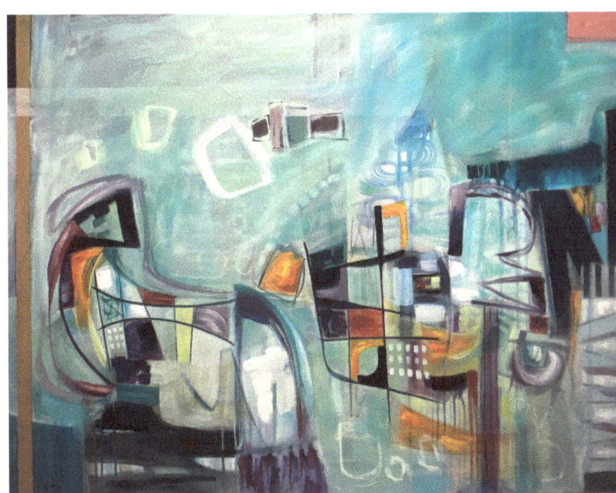

On a Rainy Day
36x48 acrylic on canvas

Benefits of Using a Limited Color Palette

There are many benefits in using a limited color palette. First, if you are branding your art, this is a benefit as it is one additional way of helping others recognize your art as "yours." It's also helpful if you are working on a collection or series and are trying to achieve a cohesive body of work. Additionally, a limited palette will help you naturally create harmonious paintings.

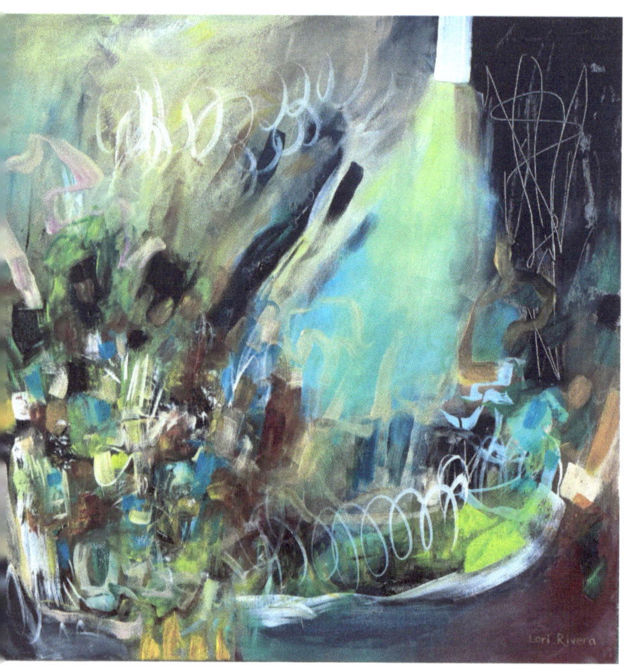

Autumn's Swirling Winds
24x24 acrylic on canvas

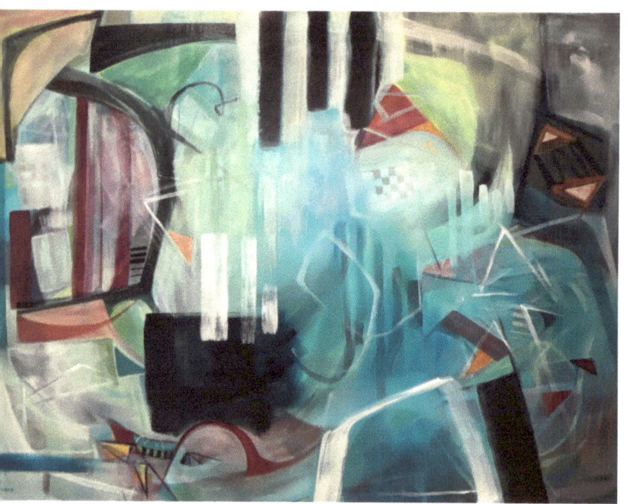

Caught in a Landslide
36x48 acrylic on canvas

With a limited palette, you have less paints to purchase. There's no guesswork on which paint colors you need to buy when you use a limited palette. I used to use 15+ different tube paint colors and would always try to replace all of them when they ran out, which meant any trip to the art store to purchase paint would be an expensive one. I also never mixed my colors, other than when they haphazardly mixed on the canvas. You can tell a difference between my early work and my most recent work. There's simply an added element of quality to my more recent work.

However, I've recently been adding more colors to my palette, as I mentioned earlier. I usually start off with a limited palette, then add 2-3 Master's Touch colors.

Another benefit of using a limited palette is that you'll find it easier to match colors. When I paint my pieces, I extend the composition of the piece to the edges of the canvas. I paint the edges as I'm painting the rest of the piece, but sometimes I miss places on the bottom and top edges, and I don't get around to painting those sides until later. With a limited palette, I'm able to quickly identify which colors are needed to mix to match the painting.

Mixing Colors Straight on the Surface

You can mix colors on your palette or straight on the surface -- canvas, paper, wood, or another substrate. If you want to mix your colors right on the canvas, you can try my method. Apply the paint with a palette knife, then grab a different color of paint on your brush and mix it in with the paint you applied with the palette knife on your canvas by dragging the brush through the edge of the paint you applied with the palette knife.

On the next several pages, I'm going to give you actual color palette examples that I've used in my paintings along with the mixing recipes. You can use these or use them as jumping off points to create your own custom color palettes.

Mixing Recipes

The following examples will give you some ideas of how you can mix colors to create totally new and unique colors. Try mixing two together in different amounts. Then try adding a third color and see how it changes. Make notes of the recipes of colors you like so you'll be able to mix them easily again. After a while, you'll be able to remember them without looking at the recipe. Eventually, you'll automatically know which colors to mix together.

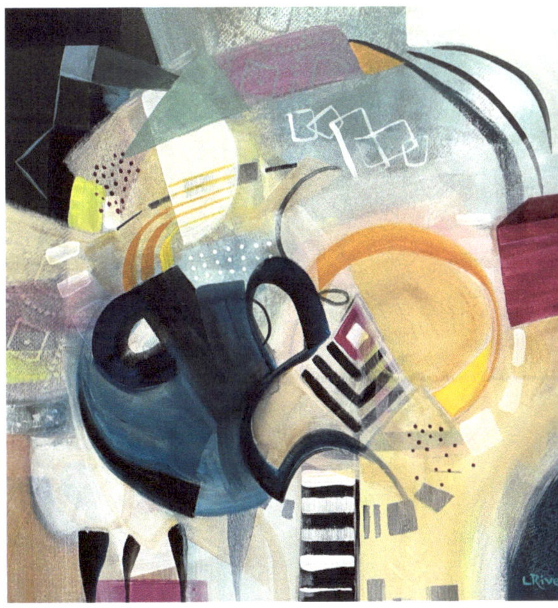

Tempest
16x16 acrylic on canvas

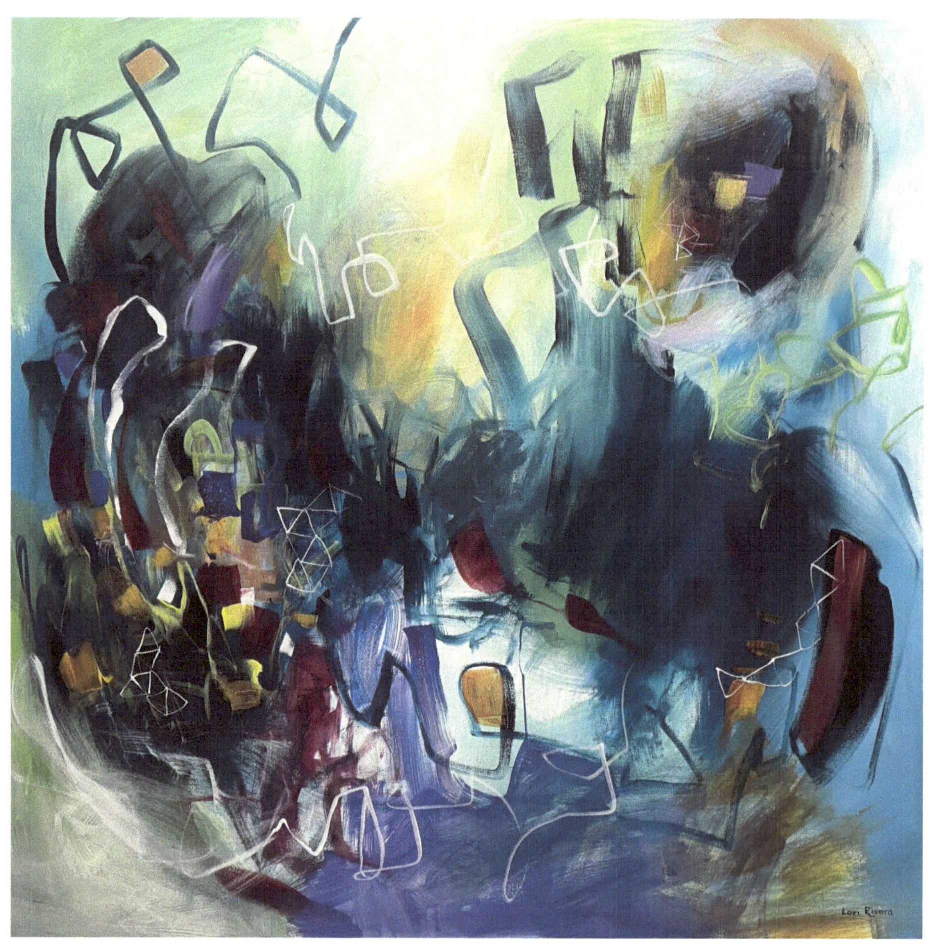

Gravity Pulling Violet*,* 36x36 acrylic on canvas

Colors needed:

Titanium White
Cadmium Yellow Light
Quinacridone Magenta
Phthalo Blue
Burnt Sienna

Mixing recipes:

Violet: equal amounts of phthalo blue + magenta
Dark blue-green color: equal amounts of phthalo blue + burnt sienna
Red: magenta + small amount of cadmium yellow
Orange: cadmium yellow + very small amount of magenta
Light green: cadmium yellow + white + small amount of phthalo blue

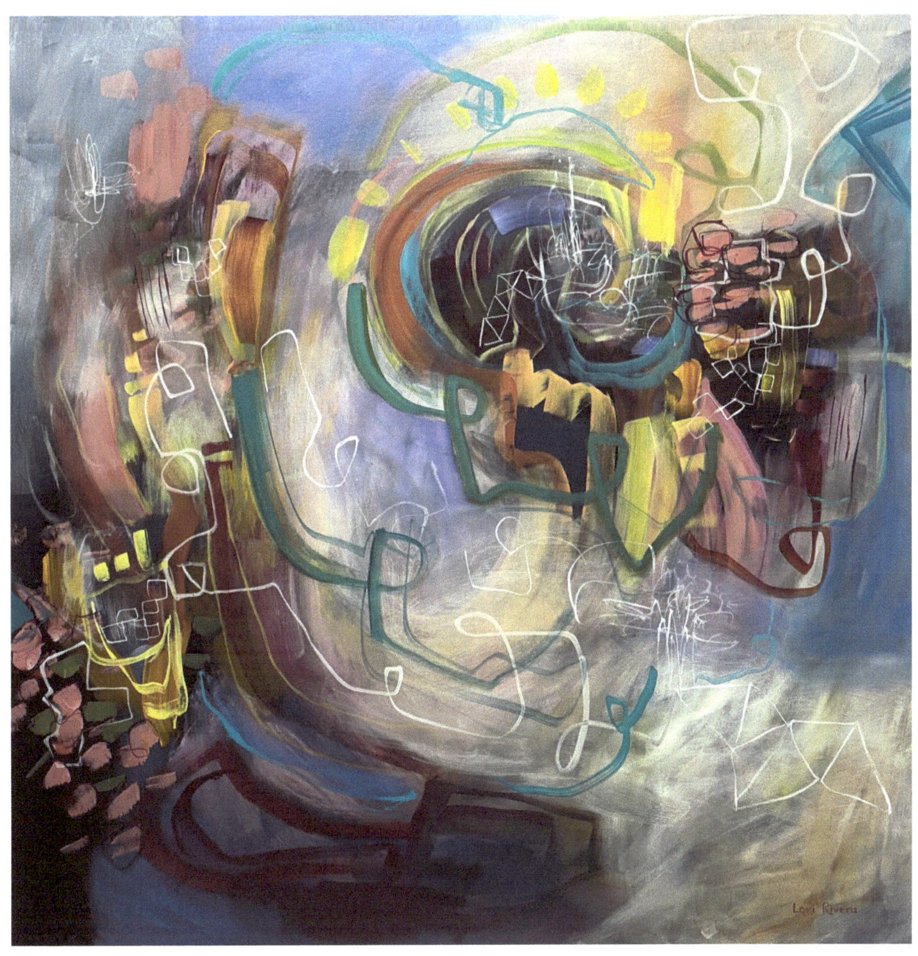

Saturday Morning, 36x36 acrylic on canvas

Colors needed:

Titanium White
Cadmium Yellow Light
Quinacridone Magenta
Phthalo Blue
Ultramarine Blue
Burnt Sienna

Mixing recipes:

Teal: phthalo blue + tiny amount of cadmium yellow, + small amount of white
Red: magenta + small amount of cadmium yellow
Yellow: cadmium yellow + white
Peach: magenta + yellow + white
Orange: magenta + yellow
Black: equal amounts of ultramarine blue + burnt sienna
Mauve: magenta + small amount of yellow + white

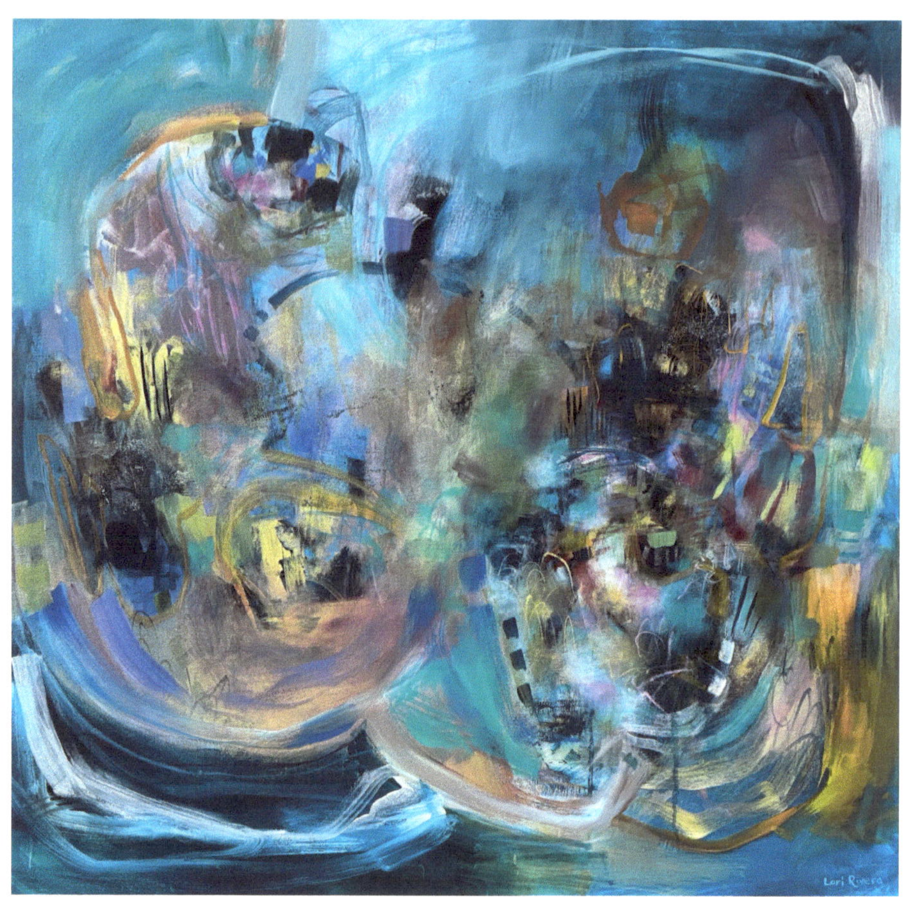

Whirl, 36x36 acrylic on canvas

Colors needed:

Titanium White
Cadmium Yellow Light
Quinacridone Magenta
Phthalo Blue
Burnt Sienna
Gold - straight out of the tube

Mixing recipes:

Turquoise: phthalo blue + tiny amount of yellow + small amount of white
Orange: magenta + yellow
Pink: magenta + white
Olive green: phthalo blue + yellow + tiny amount of magenta
Black: phthalo blue + burnt sienna

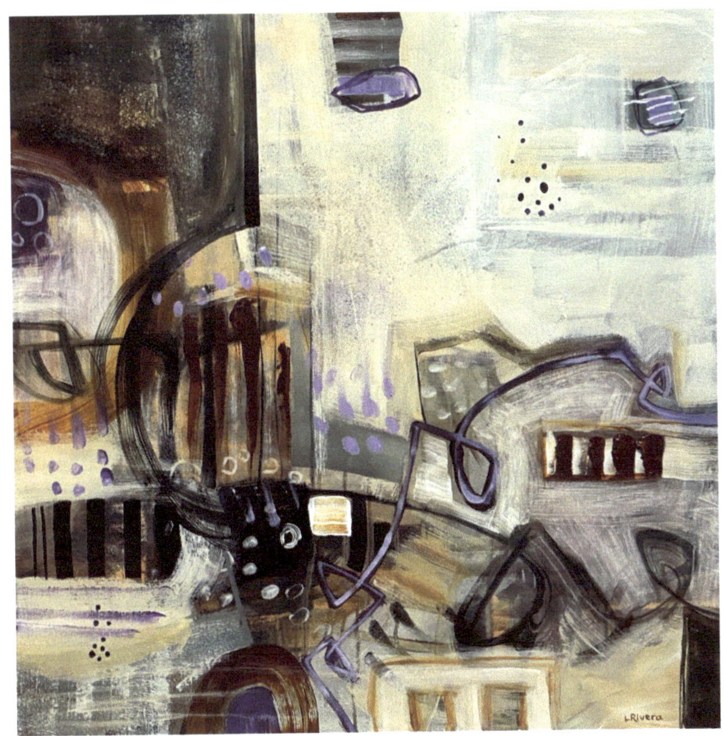

Are You Ready for It? 24x24 acrylic on canvas

TIP: *When you mix many colors together, especially colors opposite each other on the color wheel, you can get muddy colors. With that being said, sometimes the muddy colors make the best neutrals for your pieces!*

Using Neutrals to Make Colors Pop

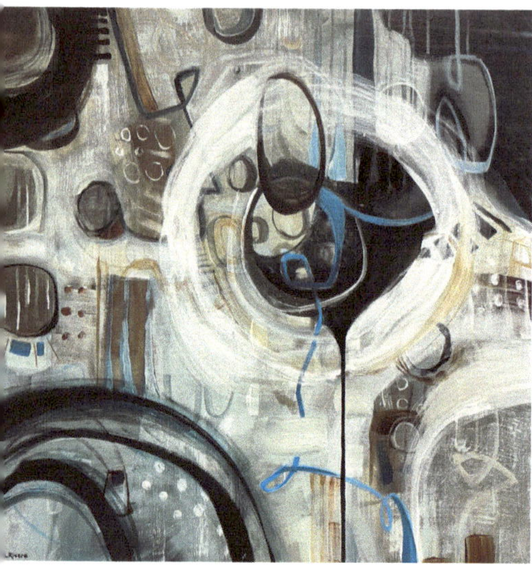

Onward
24x24 acrylic on canvas

For the longest time I just placed a bunch of bright colors together in my abstracts. Colors can look much more vibrant when placed near neutrals. Lately, I've been experimenting with using more neutral colors in my abstracts, and on this page are some examples. I have lots of neutrals in these with little pops of color.

My next goal is to create a series of abstracts using neutrals with pops of color, but I'd like to have a little more color in them then these have.

Let me demonstrate how neutrals affect bright colors. Doesn't the pink look the most vibrant when placed next to the neutral gray, versus down below by the various bright colors?

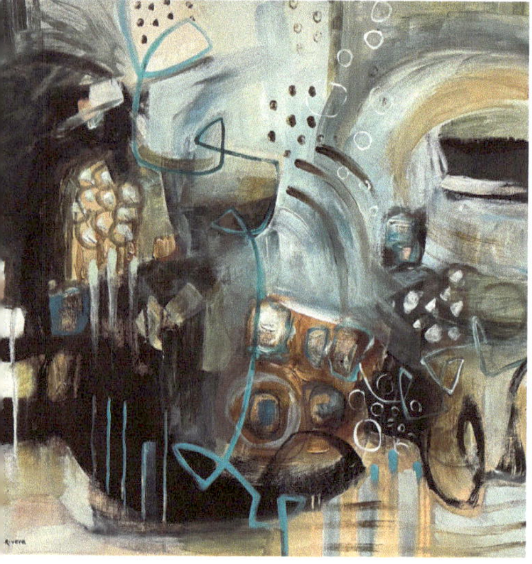

You Can Go Your Own Way
24x24 acrylic on canvas

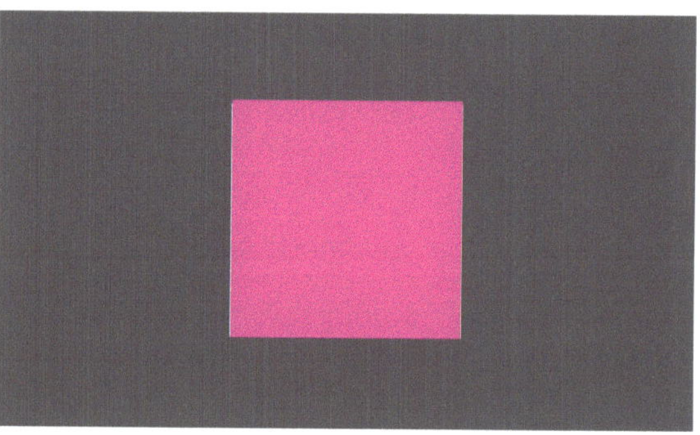

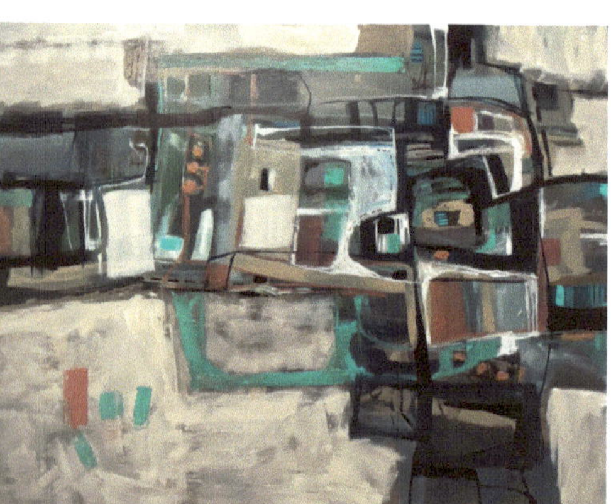

Outside These Walls
36x48 acrylic on canvas

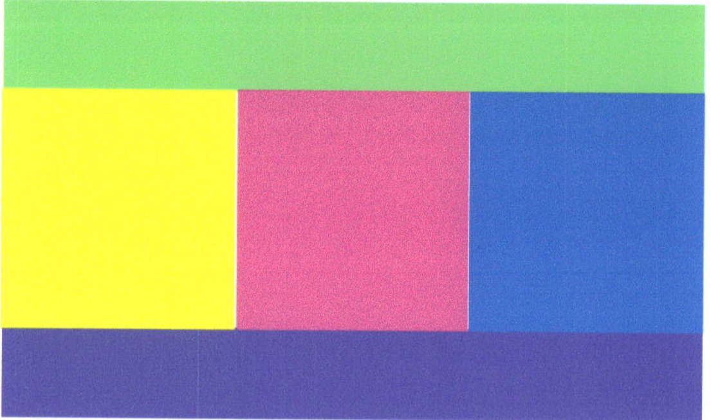

Exercises

Detecting Values

Get every tube of paint you own and paint a small (about one inch) swatch of color of each of your paints on a piece of paper or a small canvas panel. Take a photo and convert the photo to grayscale on your phone. Now compare each swatch to your tubes of paint? Are you surprised how some of the color's values are so similar?

Practicing Value Contrast

Create a monochromatic painting with just one color, while using white to lighten it and black to darken it. You'll be using tints and shades of one color along with the saturated color by itself to practice recognizing values. When in actual practice, I recommend darkening your colors with a dark color other than black, such as dark blue, dark brown, or dark purple.

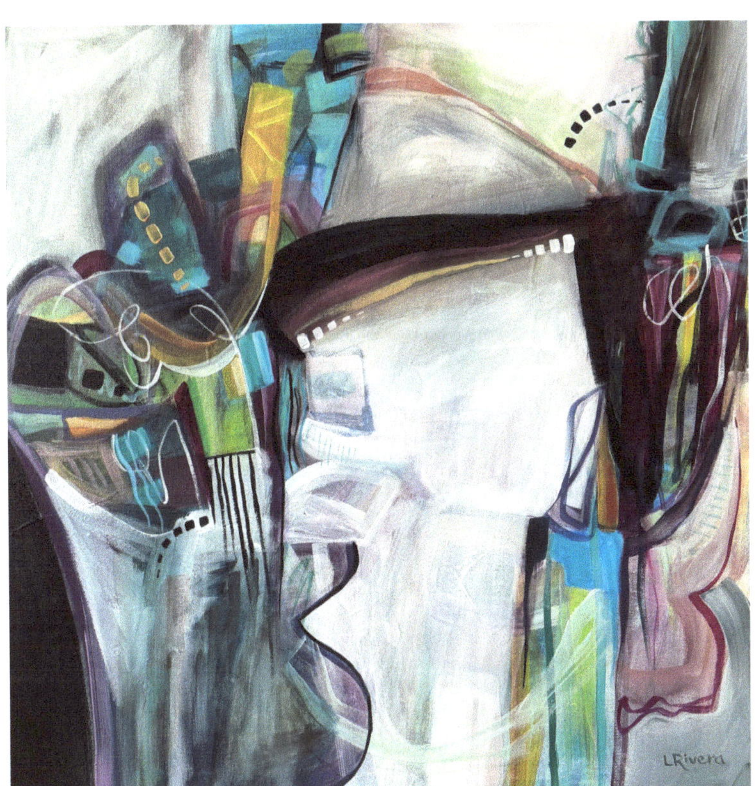

Celebrate
20x20 acrylic on canvas

Chapter 5: Mark-Making Techniques

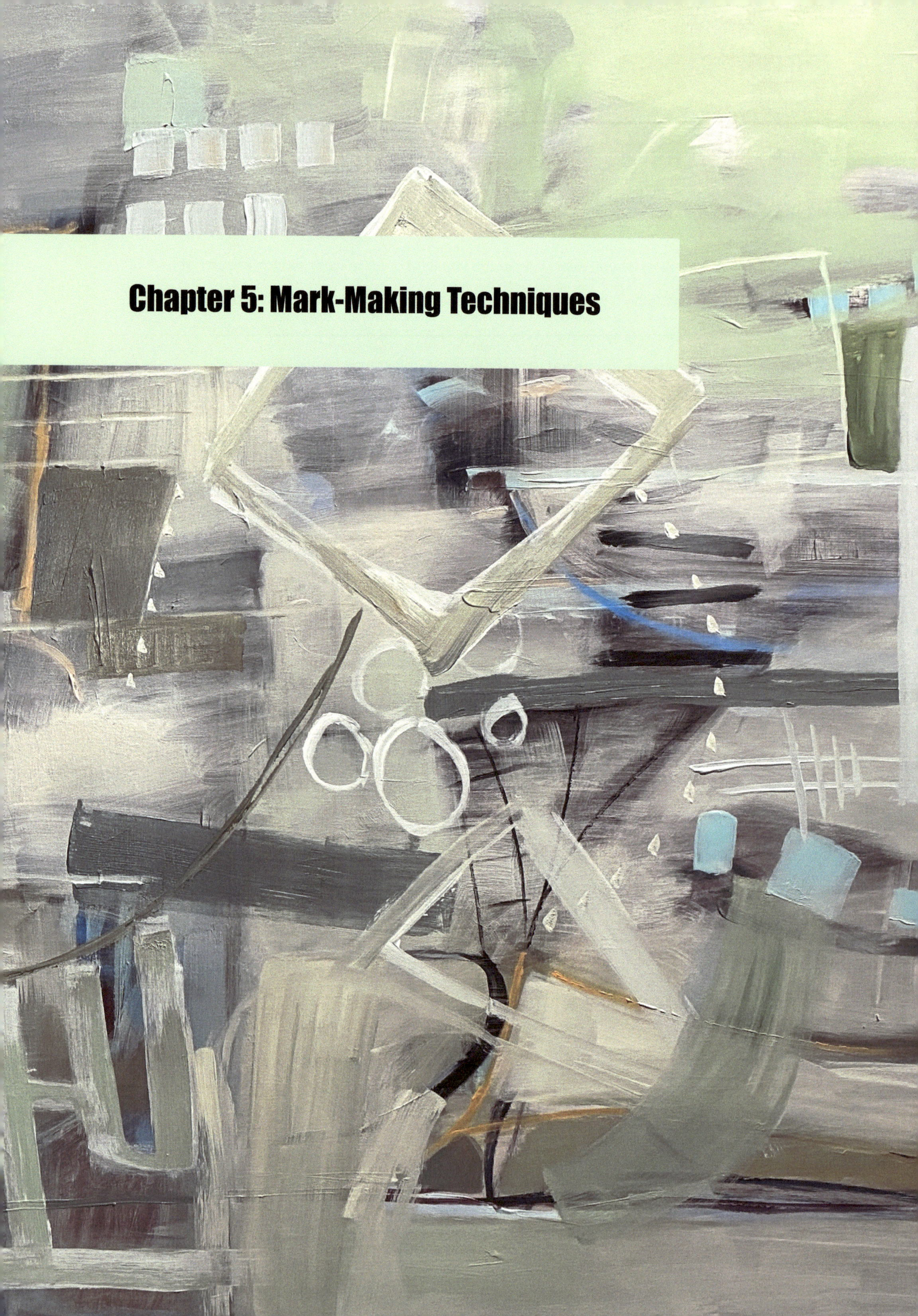

Mark-Making

Mark-making has been around since the beginning of humankind. Mark-making satisfies our primal need to express ourselves, and whether it's through writing a letter by hand or painting an abstract work of art, mark making is an integral part of our lives.

Mark-making can be controlled (tight) or it can be free (loose). I prefer loose marks, but in art there's no right or wrong, really; it's just whatever you prefer. An artist who was a natural at amazing mark-making was Cy Twombly (1928-2011). If you look him up, you'll see that his work is very playful and full of gestural marks.

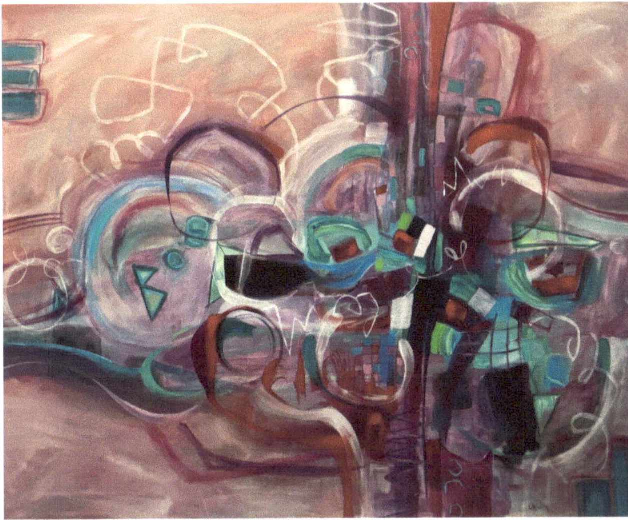

I Know It's Getting Late
36x48 acrylic on canvas

Marks can be categorized based on shape, pressure or thickness, and color. I like categorizing mark-making into feminine and masculine also. Squares, for example, can connote masculinity, and circles and curvy marks can symbolize femininity. The pressure applied in mark-making (light or heavy) can also be categorized as feminine or masculine. Light marks I consider to be more feminine, and dark and dramatic marks I like to categorize as masculine. A mark can be a blend of masculine and feminine, as in the case of a thick, dark circle, or a light, thin square. As in finished works of art, mark-making is open to interpretation, but this is how I categorize marks. Think of the above ways of categorizing mark-making when communicating messages with your art. It's all open to interpretation, so if you interpret differently than I do, that's perfectly fine, because art speaks to each of us differently.

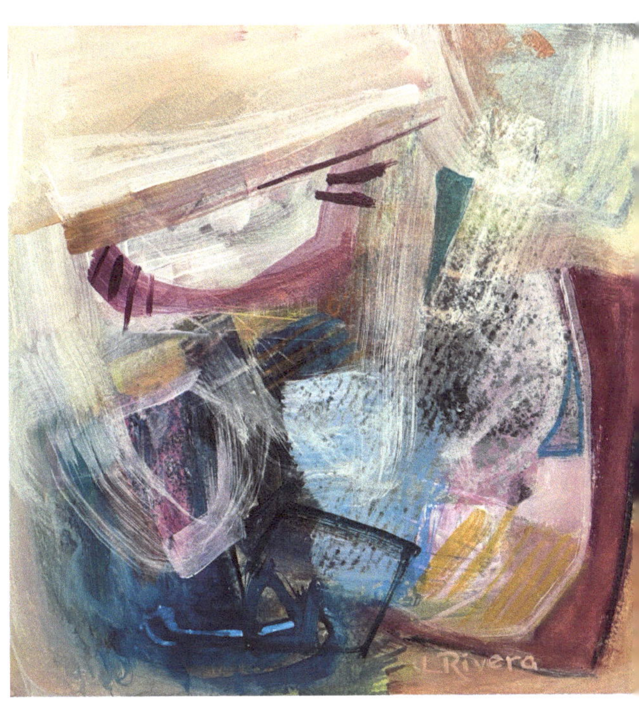

Raising the Bar
8x8 acrylic on paper

Recently, I created a collection of paintings titled

"Overload." The mark that unified all of the pieces was a rainbow inspired shape. Having mark-making brainstorming sessions, as I will have you do later in this book will help you identify a mark or a few marks to use in your next collection, or it may even become your signature mark. Something else to remember is that objects, such as marks on your canvas, usually look best in odd numbers.

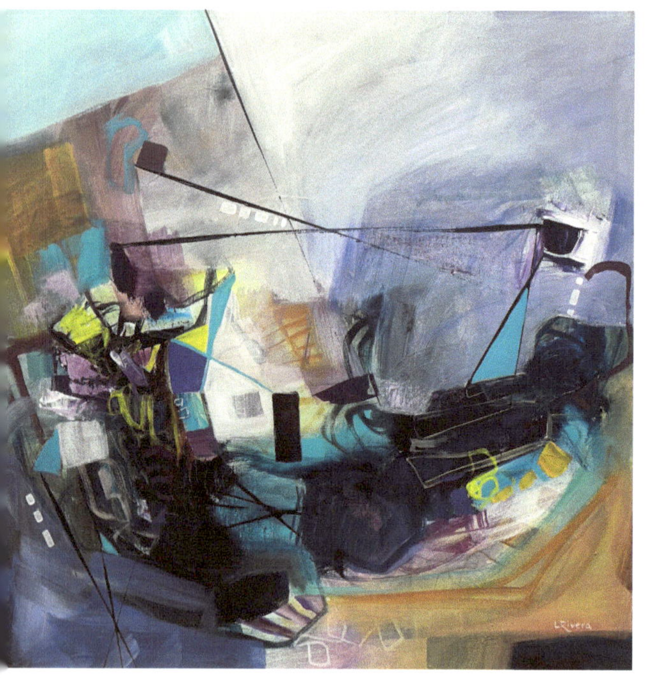

Balancing Act
24x24 acrylic on canvas

Organic vs. Geometric Marks

Mark-making can be organic or geometric. Organic marks are loose, free flowing, and asymmetrical. Geometric marks, on the other hand, are often symmetrical and can have rigid lines, such as circles, squares, hexagons, etc.

You can even take organic mark-making a bit further, to describe the process of mark-making in painting. I consider myself mostly an intuitive artist, which means that I let my intuition guide every brushstroke without a predetermined plan. If you paint in this way, you can let your marks "organically appear."

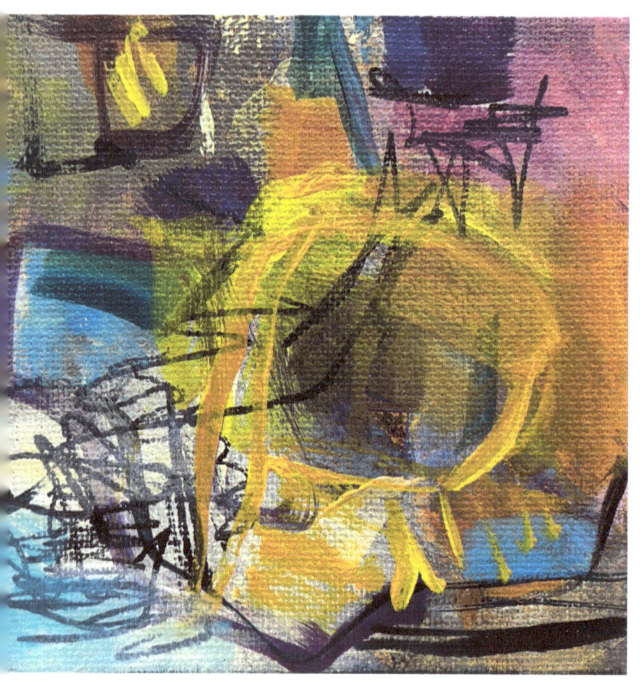

Color Splash No. 2
4x4 acrylic on canvas

Mark-making is anything you do that applies paint or another medium to the canvas, with a paintbrush, your hands, or other objects. Marks can be made with nearly any object. On the next couple of pages are some mark-making and brush techniques you can incorporate into your abstracts.

The marks you use in your paintings will help give them their personality.

Toothbrush

Adding paint on a toothbrush, directing it towards your painting, and flicking it with your fingers can create a nice effect. I've seen artists create stars in their paintings with this method, but it can also simply be used to give an implied texture to the canvas/paper.

Leaf

This is an example of a leaf impression. I applied paint to a leaf from our yard, then pressed it on the canvas.

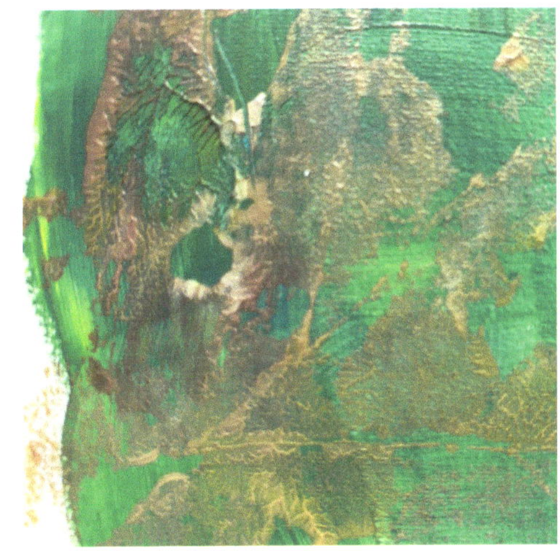

Sponge

In this example, I painted the canvas red and waited for it to dry. Then I applied light blue paint to a sponge and pressed it on the canvas.

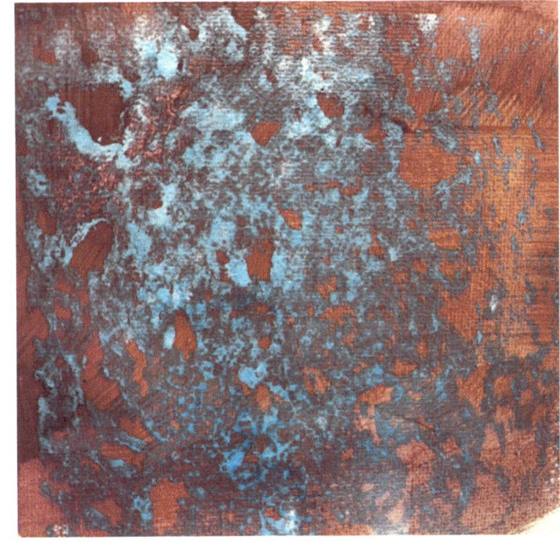

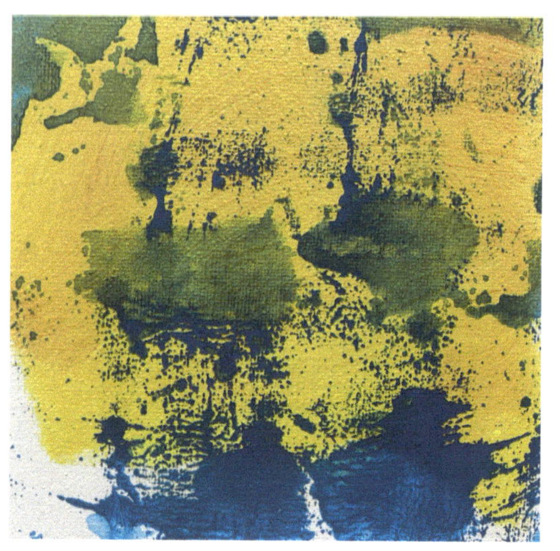

Brayer

This is what it looks like when you apply paint in different places on a brayer, then roll it on the canvas. A brayer is a small roller that is often used in printmaking. I first painted it solid yellow, then waited several minutes before I applied blue paint unevenly to the brayer and rolled it on the canvas.

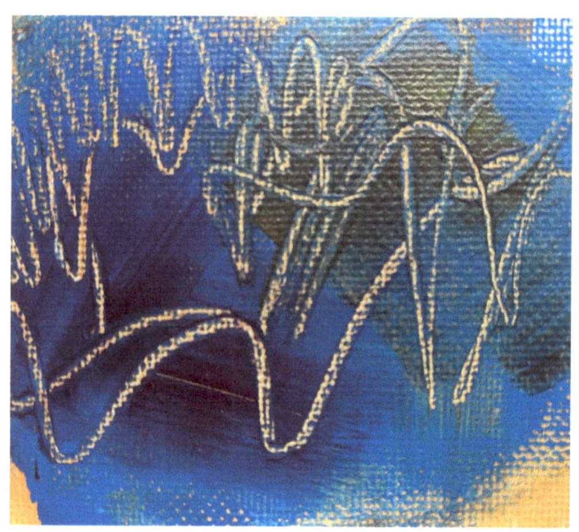

Scraping with a Palette Knife

I took a palette knife and scraped the blue paint while it was wet to reveal the underneath layer.

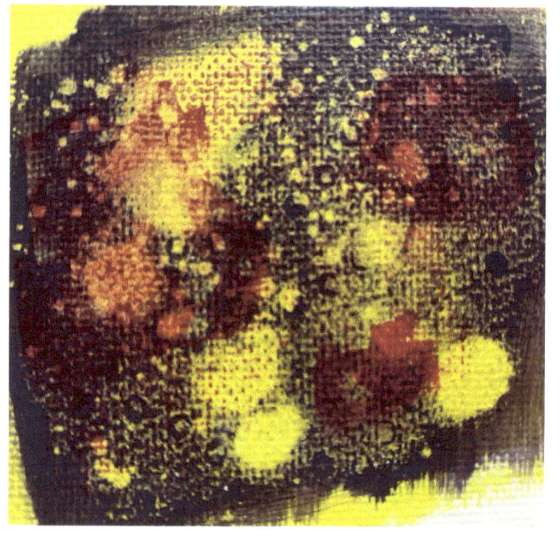

Paper Towel Lift

In this example, I painted the surface yellow. I let the yellow dry, then added purple and red. Then I let the purple and red set for about two minutes, then sprayed the area with a spray bottle. I waited another couple minutes, then I took a paper towel and pressed on the paint for about 30 seconds, then pulled the paper towel away.

Dry Brush

If your underneath layer is dry, then you can take a dry brush and dip it into paint, then add some brushstrokes. This is the effect you will get.

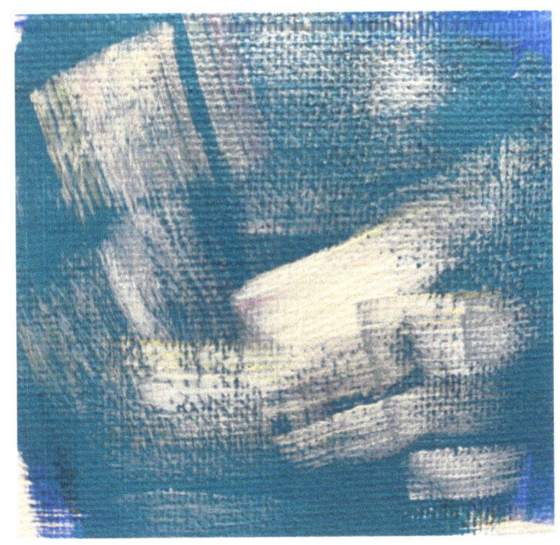

Palette Knife Painting

I applied paint with a palette knife in this picture. First red, then blue over the red. You can get wonderful impasto (thick paint) effects with palette knives and there are tons of sizes of knives to choose from.

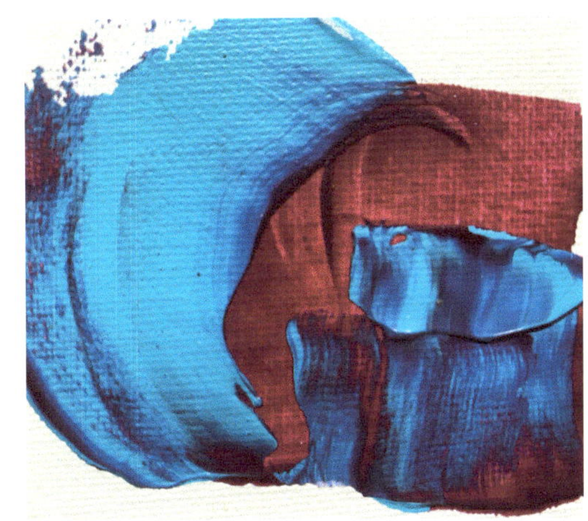

Blending

In this example, I blended turquoise and yellow. You can do this by sweeping your brush back and forth between the two colors.

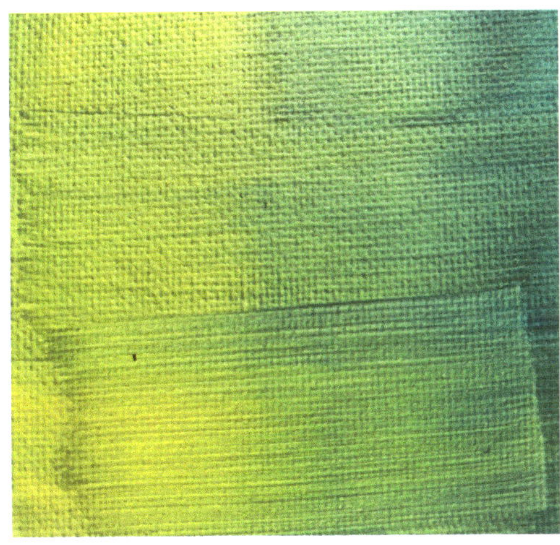

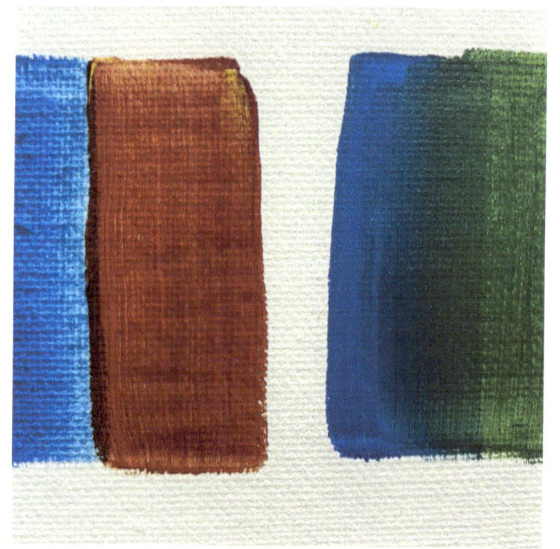

Hard and Soft Edges

You can have both hard edges (left) and soft edges (right). With soft edges you blend the colors a little, and hard edges are created by placing two colors next to one another but not mixing them together.

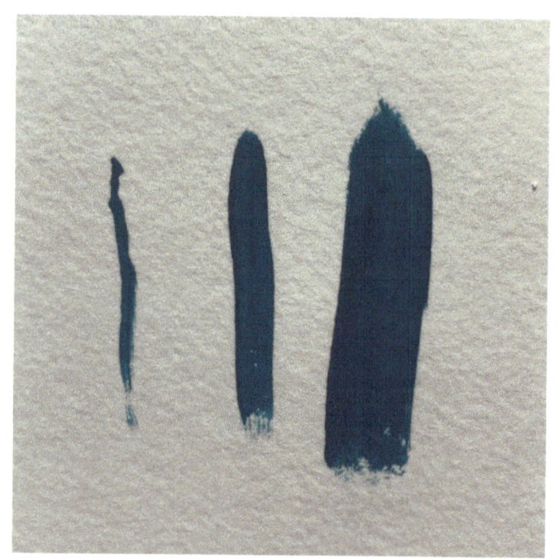

Varying the Pressure with Your Paintbrush

You'll find that you can get drastically different marks from the same paintbrush if you vary the pressure. These three marks were created with a small round brush using varying degrees of pressure.

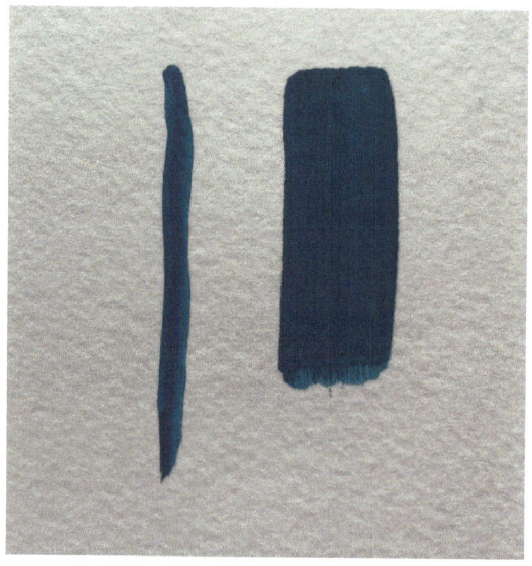

Turning Brush 90 Degrees

You'll also find that you can get different marks from paintbrushes by rotating them 90 degrees. These marks where created with a small flat paintbrush, the left one on its edge.

To the right are some additional examples of mark-making. Marks can be anything you want them to be, and you'll find over time that you'll probably gravitate towards certain ones, which may even become your signature marks.

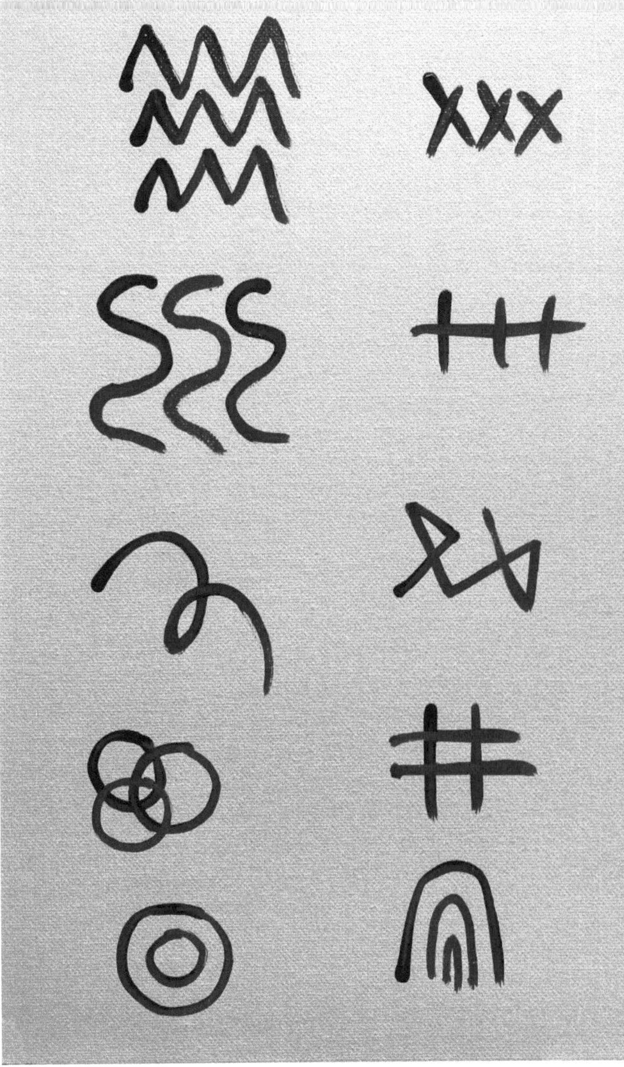

A Short Note on Commissions

I usually don't have any idea what marks I will use in a painting as I don't plan my pieces, unless I'm painting a commission. I find abstract commissions to be somewhat challenging due to my intuitive painting process. Clients usually have something in mind of how they want the final piece to look, which requires a little bit of planning on my part.

I find the ArtRage app to be helpful in planning my commission pieces. After I get the first few layers done and get to a good point, I show the client what I have so far. If they want changes, I can test out the changes in the ArtRage app before making changes to the actual piece.

If you'd like to take my ArtRage class, just go to https://bit.ly/ArtRageTutorial

Exercise

Take a 9x12 or larger canvas panel and make as many marks as you can think of (trying some of the ones in this chapter and some of your own). This is like a painting brainstorming session. Anything goes. Don't filter anything. Try anything that comes to mind. Which marks do you like and which ones do you not like? Keep this canvas panel for future reference. You may also want to label each one and how it was created.

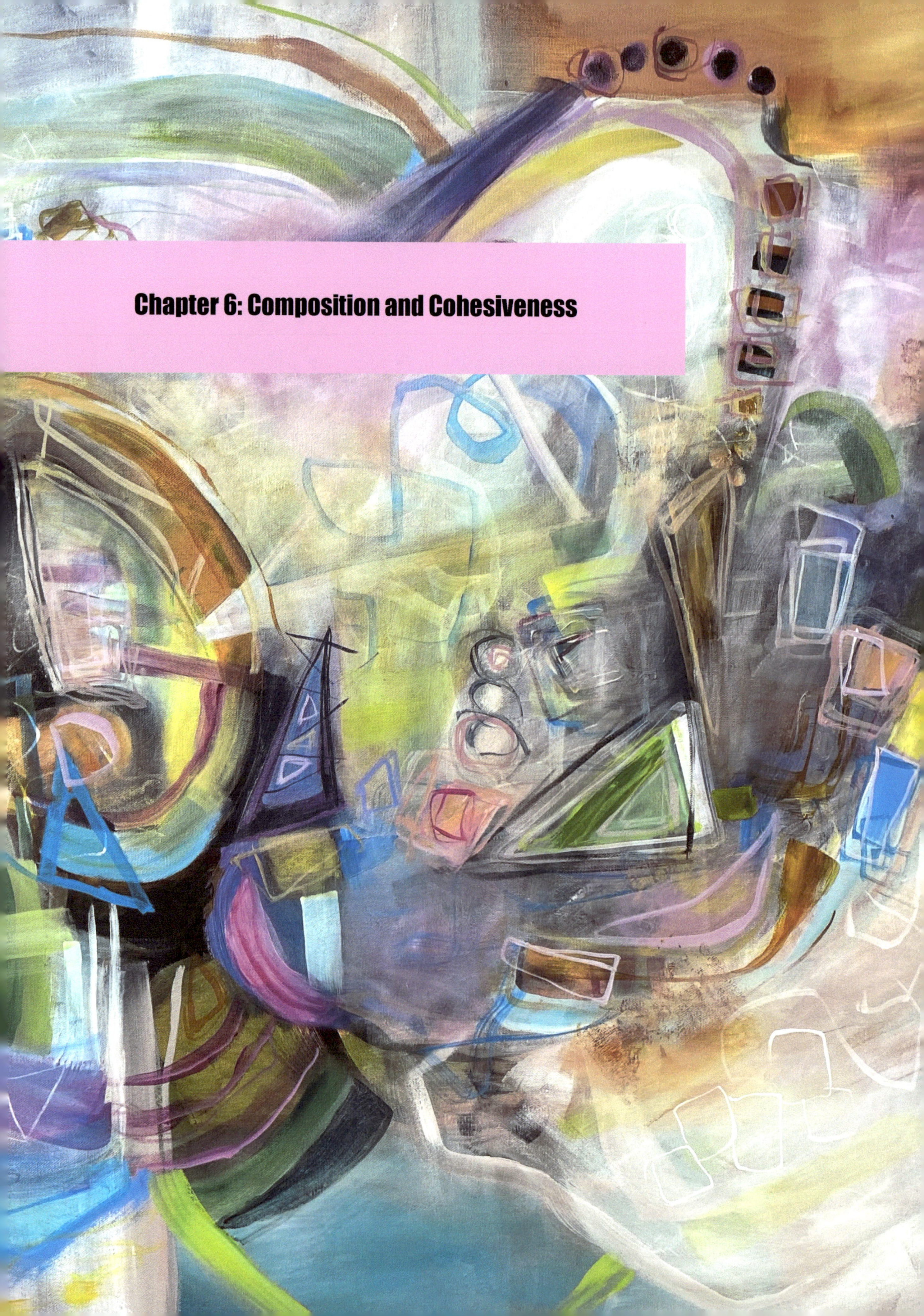

Chapter 6: Composition and Cohesiveness

Composition and Cohesiveness

Composition is how you arrange your painting and is probably what's noticed first in a painting. Your goal for your painting will determine what type of composition you use.

If your purpose is to create a calming piece, you might want to lay down calming blues and greens without much variation or energy. If your purpose is to create a feeling of energy, you might want to use a composition that draws the eye around the canvas, with several busy areas and some areas of rest. This is my favorite way to lay out a painting. Your composition will really depend on your end goal.

...if your purpose is to create a calming piece, you might want to lay down calming blues and greens without much variation or energy.

On the next couple pages are some example composition types. These are my favorite in abstract painting, and while not an exhaustive list, the possibilities are really endless. But these examples will give you jumping off points for your own paintings.

I find composition in abstract art to be the most difficult part of painting abstractly. It's probably the last aspect of abstract painting I started to understand. It becomes easier the more you practice so get out those canvases and paints and practice every chance you get!

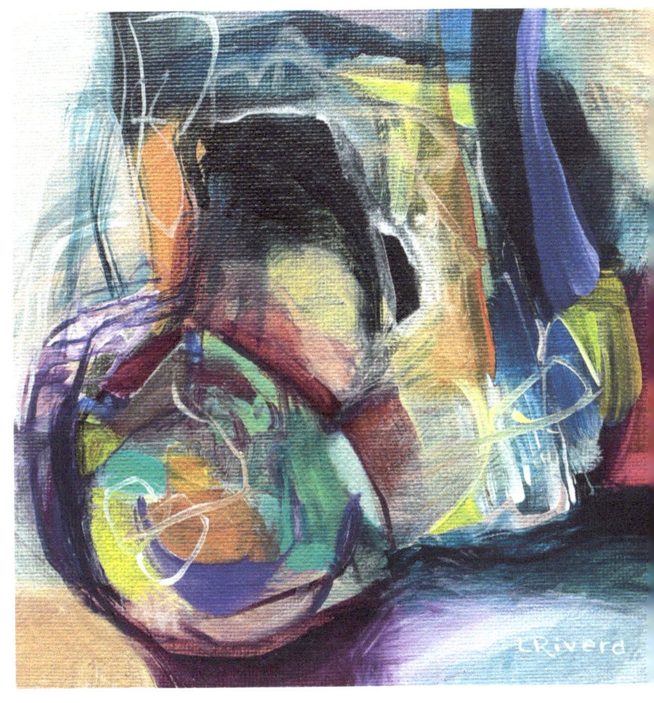

I Told You So
6x6 acrylic on canvas panel

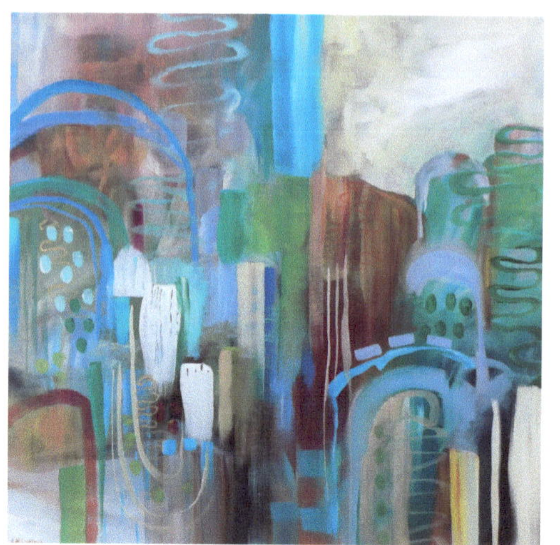

Rectangular Pattern

This is a repeating rectangular composition. I spiced this one up a bit with some semi-circular rainbow shapes as well.

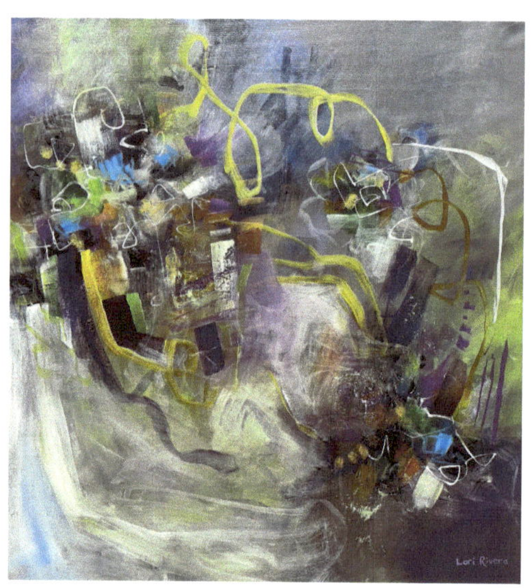

Triangular

This is a triangular composition. There are three busy areas in the painting, one at the top left, one at the bottom right, and a small busy area off to the top right. If you connect these three areas, it creates a triangle. This is one of my favorite composition types.

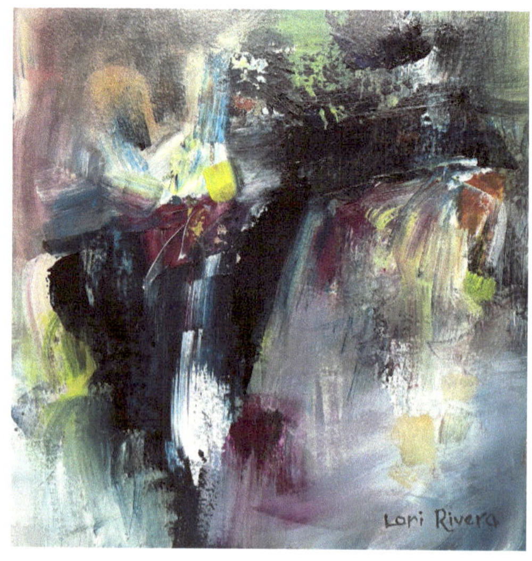

L Shape

This composition type is what it says -- it's in the shape of an L. This one is an upside down L.

Cross

This is a cross-shaped composition and is a very popular composition arrangement for abstract artists.

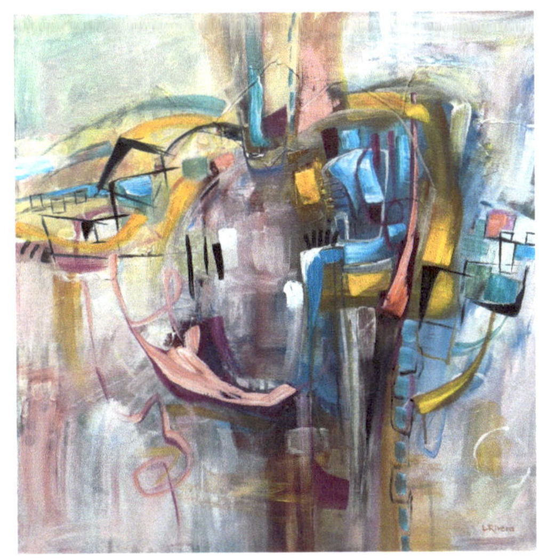

Circular

This is an example of a circular composition, and circular compositions don't necessarily have to be this obvious. If your eye is drawn into a circular pattern, it's probably a circular composition.

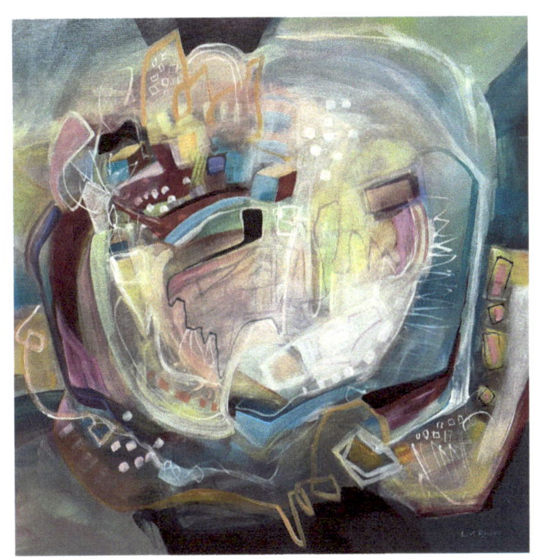

All Over

In an all over composition there is really no specified focal point, but rather elements all over the surface to draw your eye around.

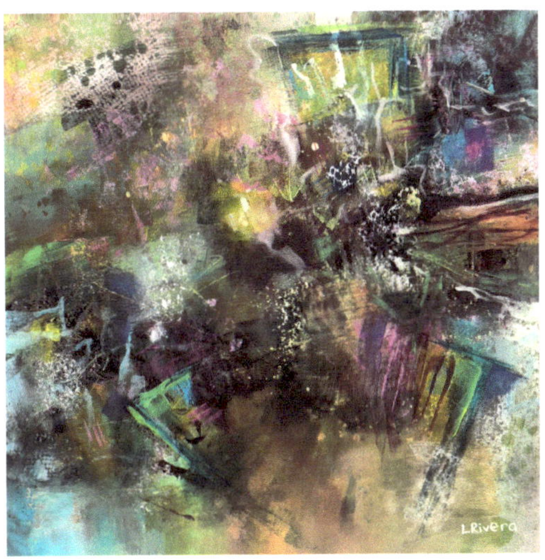

Remember that it's important to have fun when painting; it should be something you enjoy. And while a nice composition helps a piece stand on its own, remember also there are no hard and fast rules to abstract painting. The best advice, other than showing you some sample compositions, is to use your intuition and do what feels right.

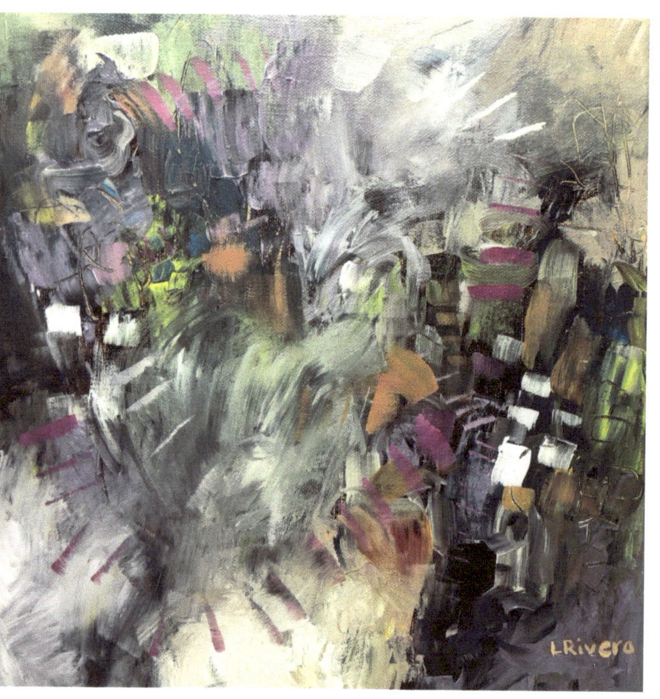

Dark of Night
12x12 acrylic on canvas

Cohesiveness

The thing that has helped me grow the most as an abstract artist in terms of learning about composition and focal points is working in a series. This has helped me create more cohesive bodies of work and has helped me develop an overall style, even though it's always evolving.

When you work in a series, you are creating a number of paintings that are related in some way, such as by color, shape, subject, composition, or another aspect.

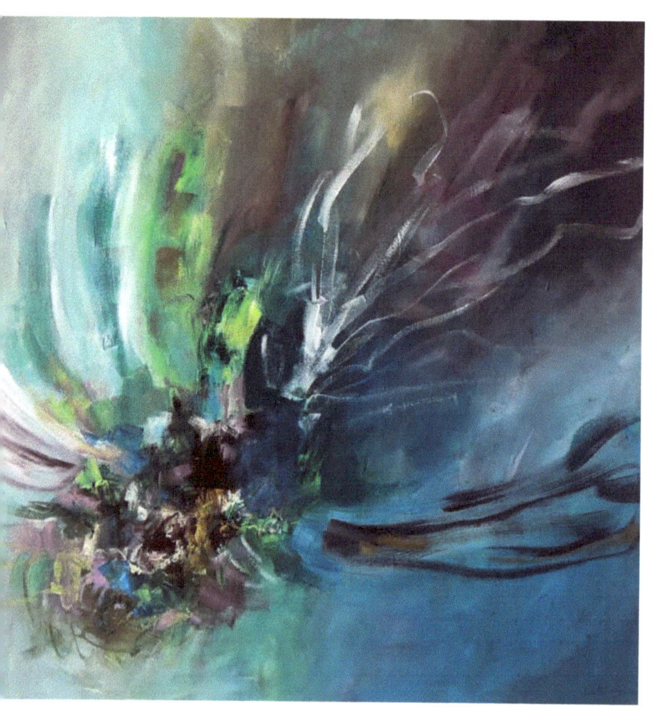

December Spritz
20x20 acrylic on canvas

If you're struggling to develop a cohesive body of work, this is definitely the route you need to take. I have much more cohesive bodies of work when I work in series. My music inspiration series is my favorite series so far.

I've also found that working small was helpful in developing more of a style. Painting small and painting often helped a lot. For almost the entire year of 2020, I created what I like to call studies, every day. I painted at least one painting each day on a 6x6 inch canvas panel. Doing this diligently for almost an entire year helped propel me forward. Then I eventually moved on to larger pieces.

Here are some examples of series I created in 2020.

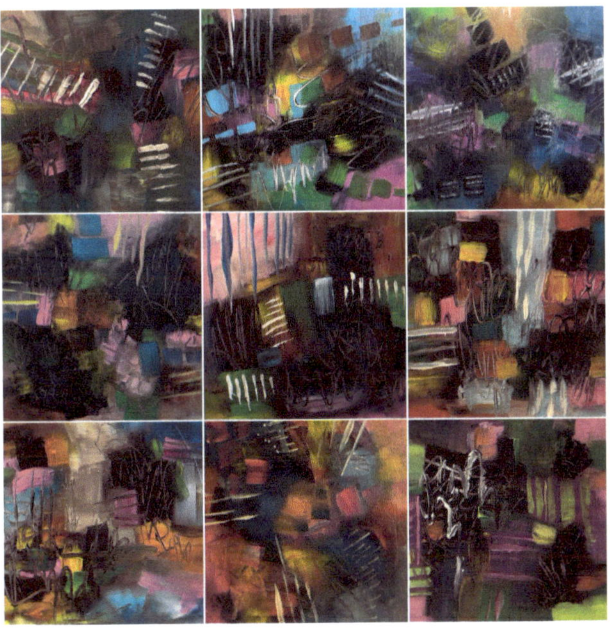

Alive Series - tied together by color
palette, composition type, and mark-making.
6x6s acrylic on panel

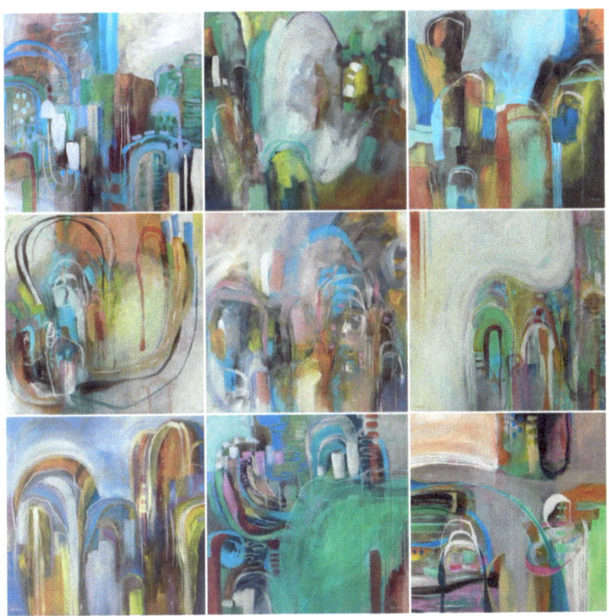

Overload Series - tied together by color palette and shape.
24x24s acrylic on canvas

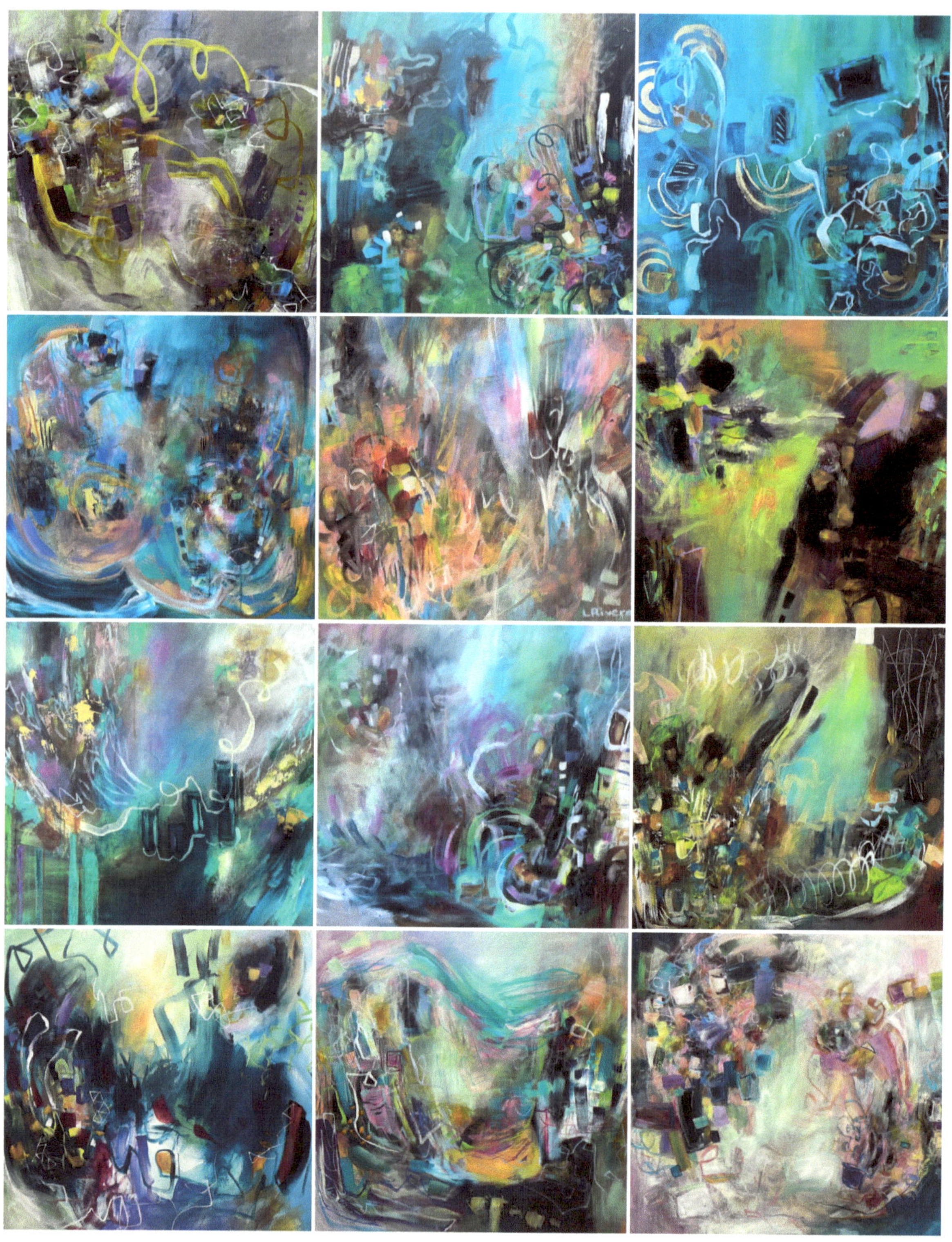

Music Inspiration Series - tied together by process and inspiration (listening to classical, jazz, hip hop, and other genres of music). Sometimes I listen to a song on repeat while painting, and other times I just listen to a certain genre. Various sizes, acrylic on canvas

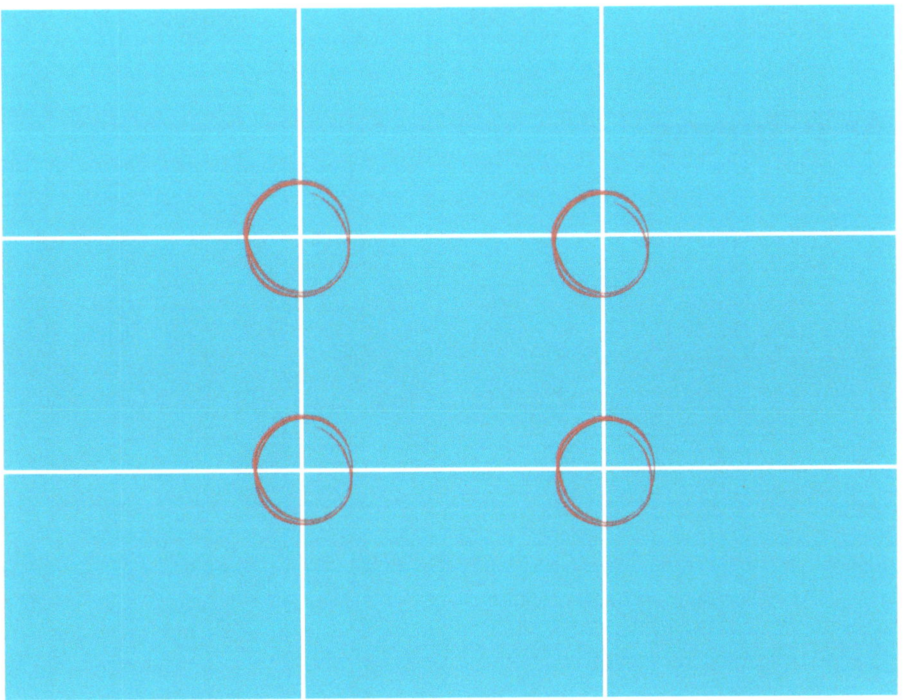

TIP: The rule of thirds is when you divide your piece into three equal parts, both vertically and horizontally. Many artists follow this rule which suggests your focal point should be on an intersection, as circled above. Your focal point is the area where you put the most emphasis and is usually the area viewers notice first. It commands the most attention.

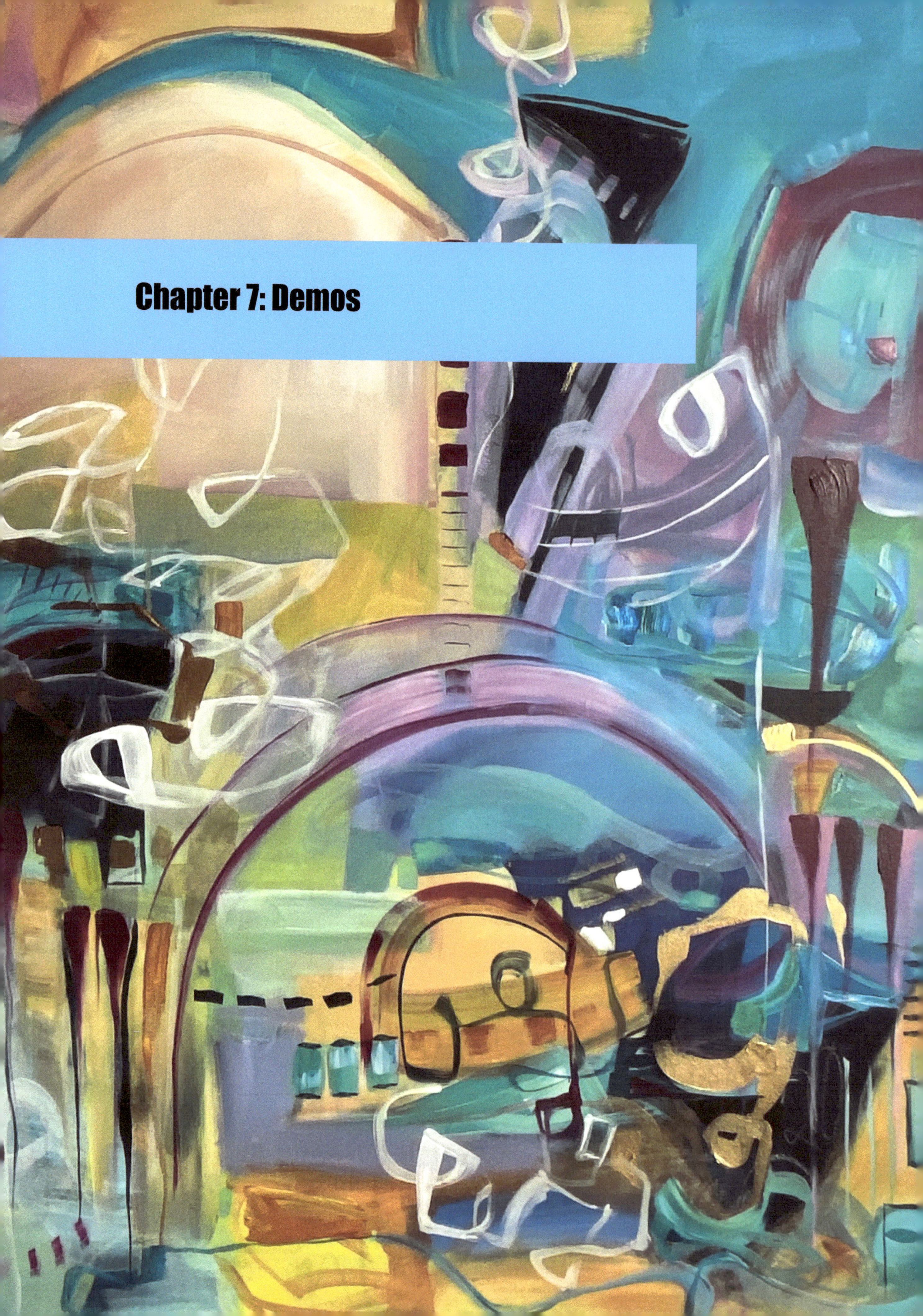

Chapter 7: Demos

My Process

Everyone has a different process, unique to that individual and how he/she works. I work with no predetermined plan and rely on intuition and spontaneity; each brushstroke guides the next. I begin each piece by toning the canvas (painting it a solid color), and while this isn't absolutely necessary in abstract painting, I find it useful. More than anything it just gives the canvas some color so it seems less intimidating to get started. Lately, however, I've been painting the first layer of my painting with several colors instead of one solid color. I just grab whatever colors feel right and cover the canvas.

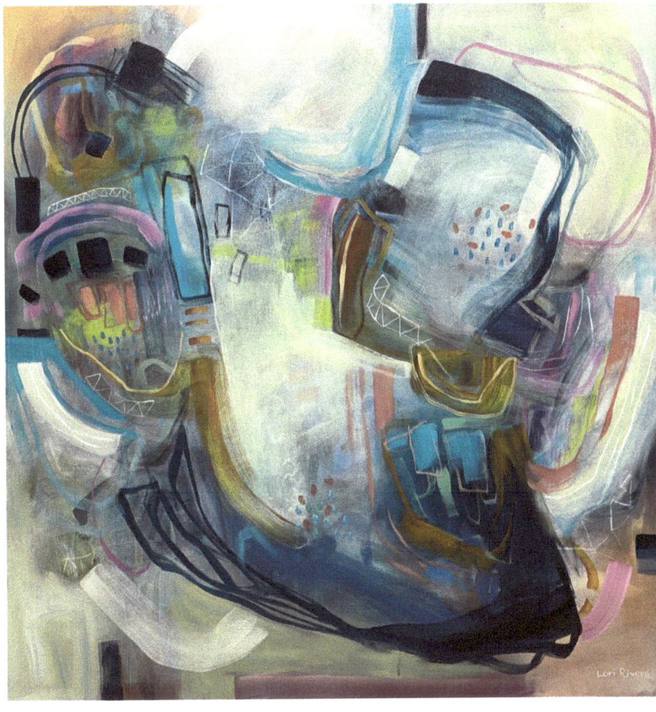

In the Quiet of the Night
36x36 acrylic on canvas

In my first layer I simply paint with freedom and create expressive marks while not giving too much thought to what I am doing at that point. I try to work very fast and loose and cover the entire canvas with large areas of color.

Very small pieces of my first layer might show up in my final piece, but this layer mostly gets covered up. I generally work dark in the beginning and work up to lighter colors, but not always. It may simply be my imagination, but this seems to help give the painting more depth.

On the next few pages, I demonstrate the process I go through in painting. You can see the progress going from top left to bottom right, with the finished piece being on the bottom right of each page.

Don't Stop the Music

36x36 acrylic on canvas

Here are the four stages of this painting

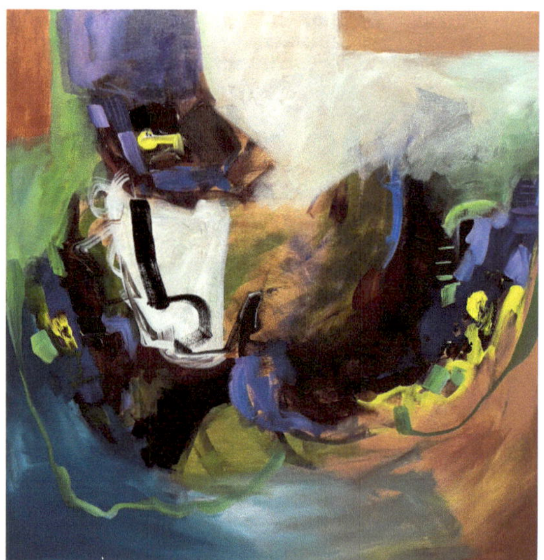

Stage 1

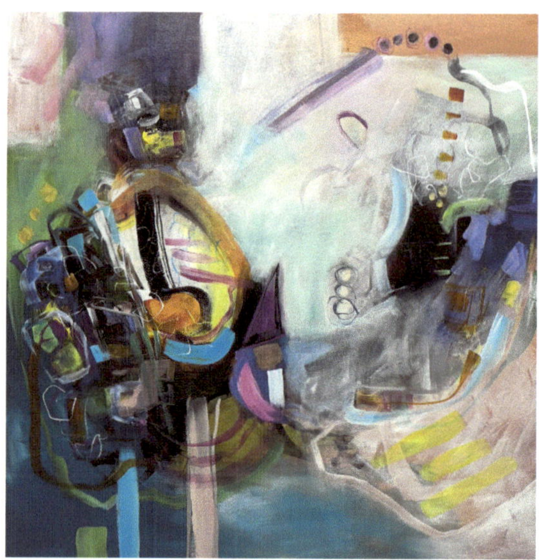

Stage 2

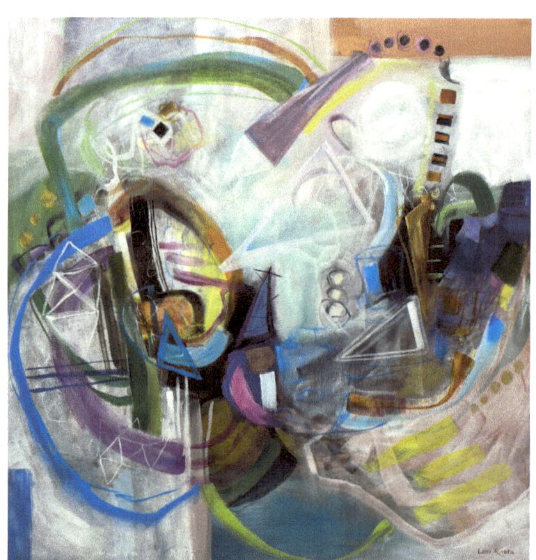

Stage 3

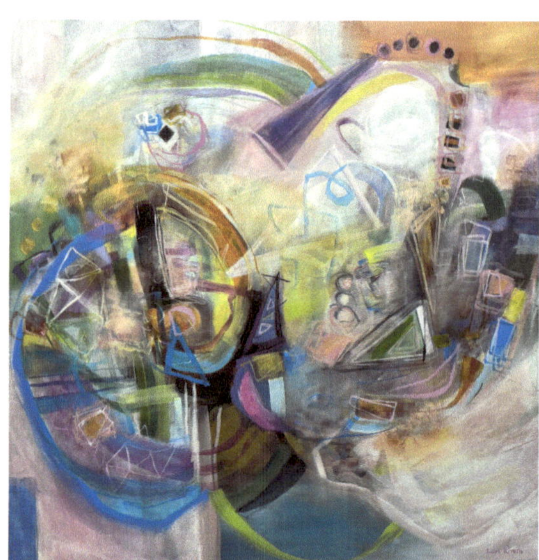

Stage 4 - final stage

Ride

20x20 acrylic on canvas

Here are the four stages of this painting

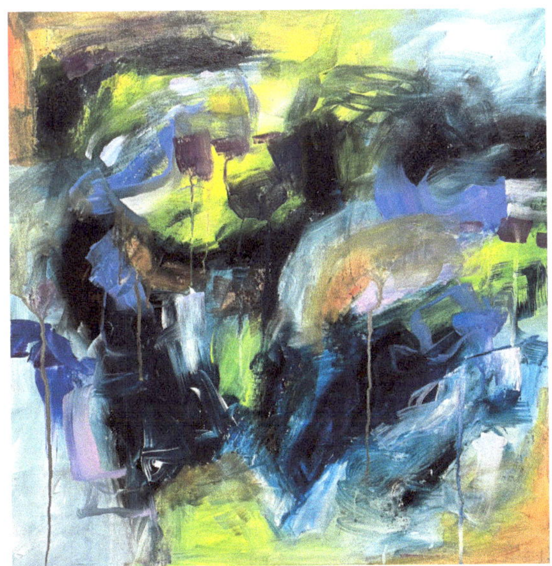

Stage 1

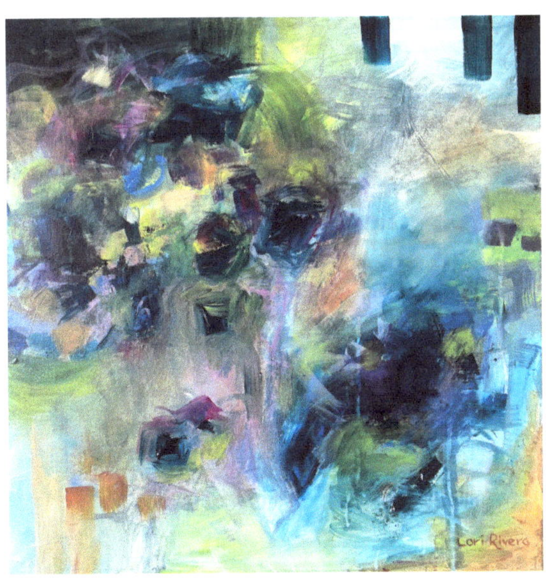

Stage 2

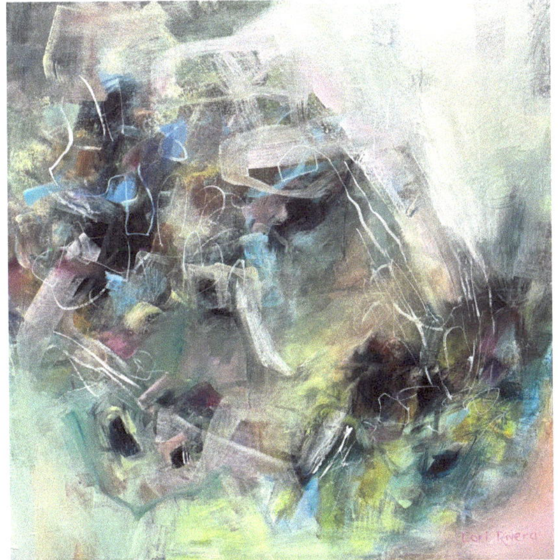

Stage 3

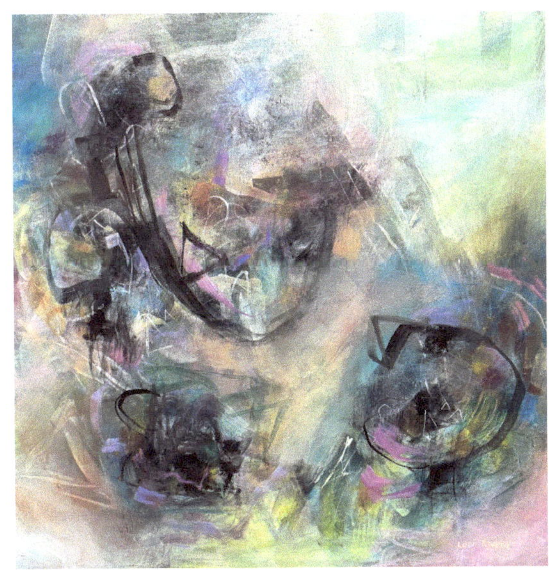

Stage 4 - final stage

Becoming Centered

36x36 acrylic on canvas

Here are the four stages of this painting

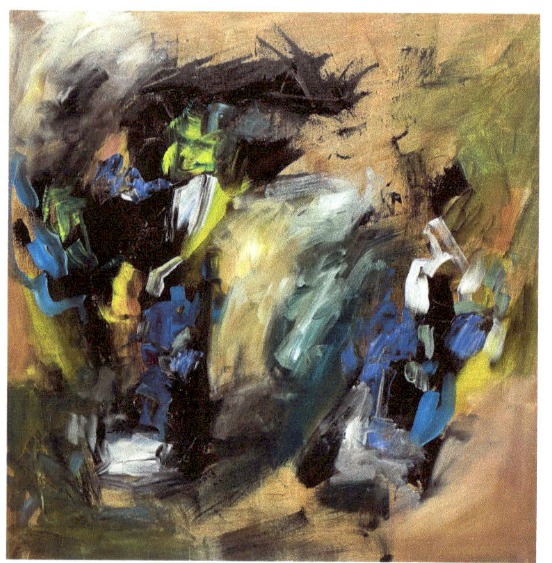

Stage 1

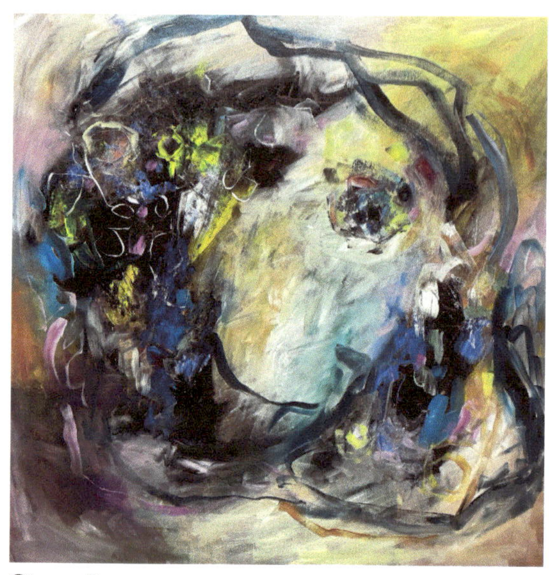

Stage 2

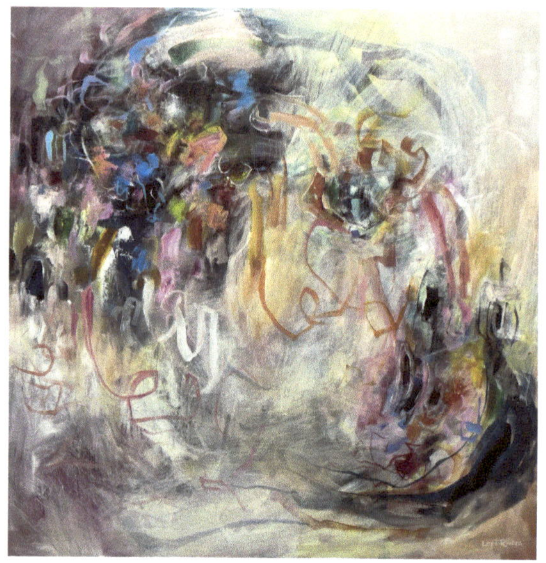

Stage 3

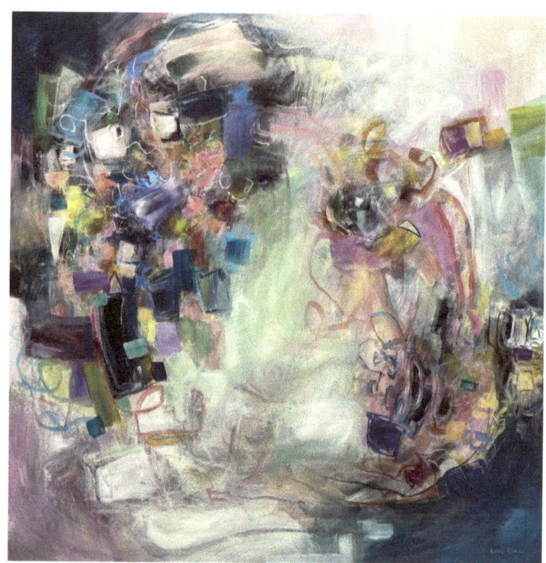

Stage 4 - final stage

Heading Northeast

36x36 acrylic on canvas

Here are the four stages of this painting

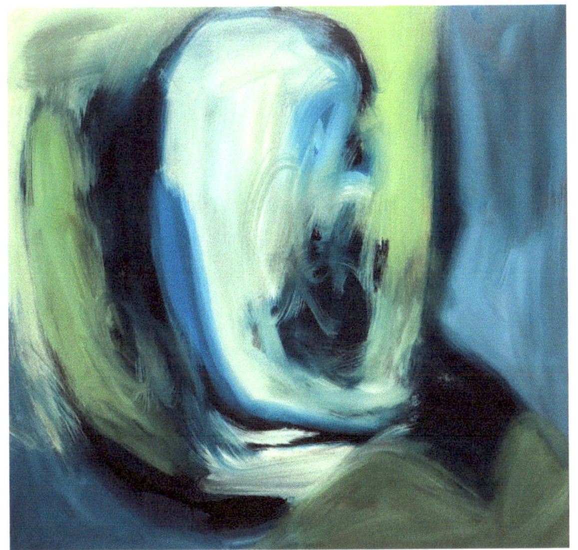

Stage 1

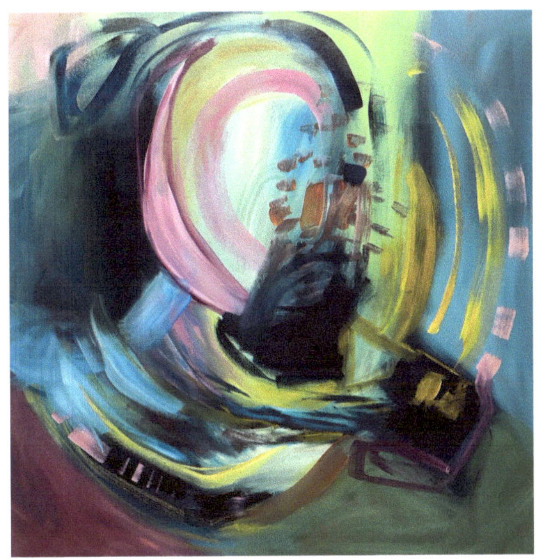

Stage 2

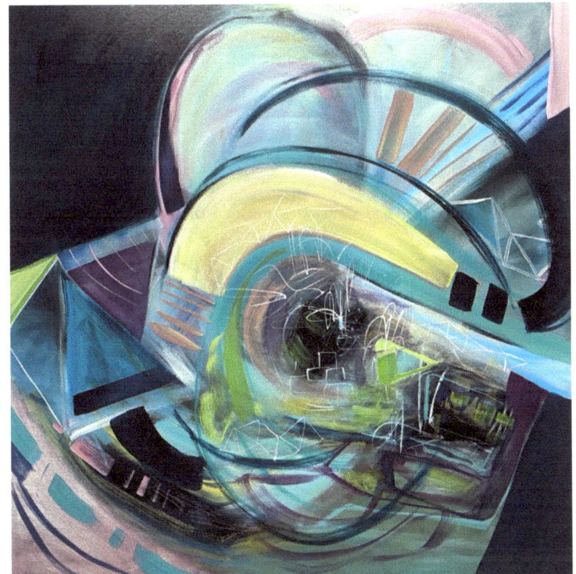

Stage 3

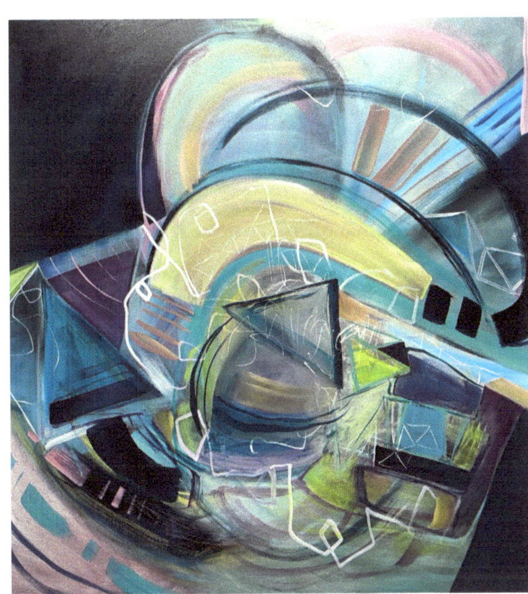

Stage 4 - final stage

Whirl

36x36 acrylic on canvas

Here are the four stages of this painting

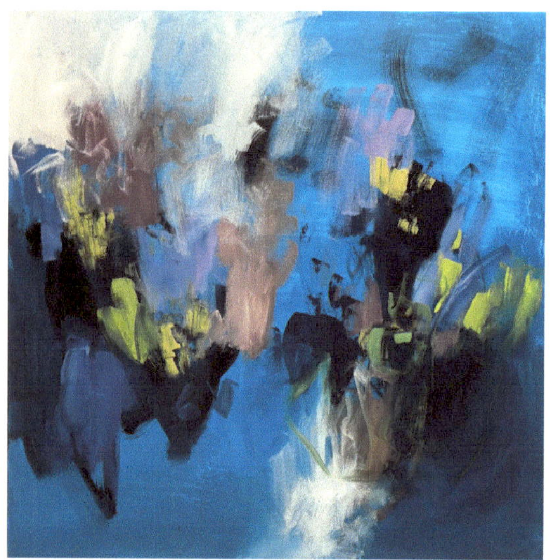

Stage 1

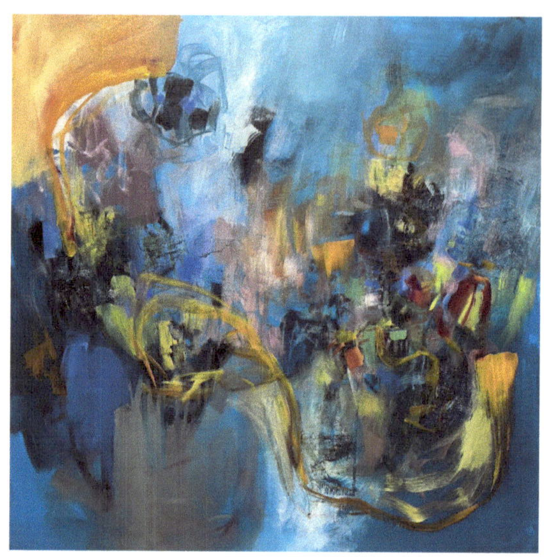

Stage 2

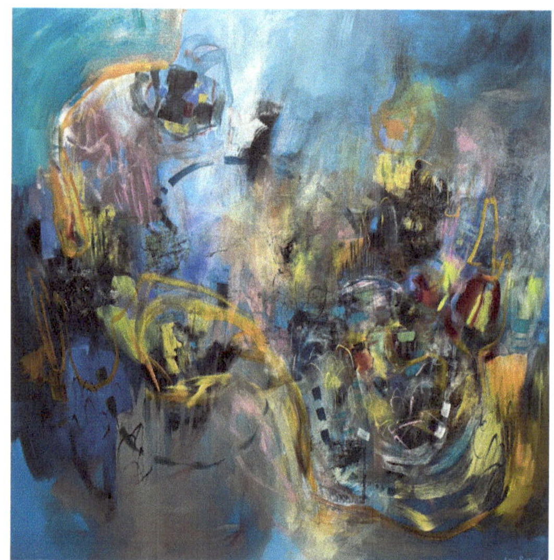

Stage 3

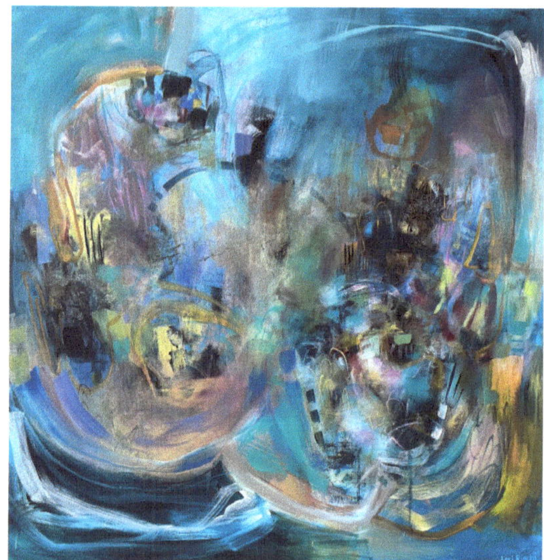

Stage 4 - final stage

In the Quiet of the Night

36x36 acrylic on canvas

Here are the four stages of this painting

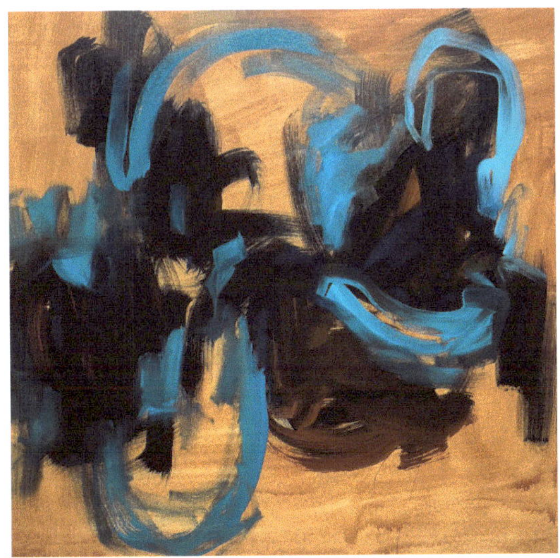

Stage 1

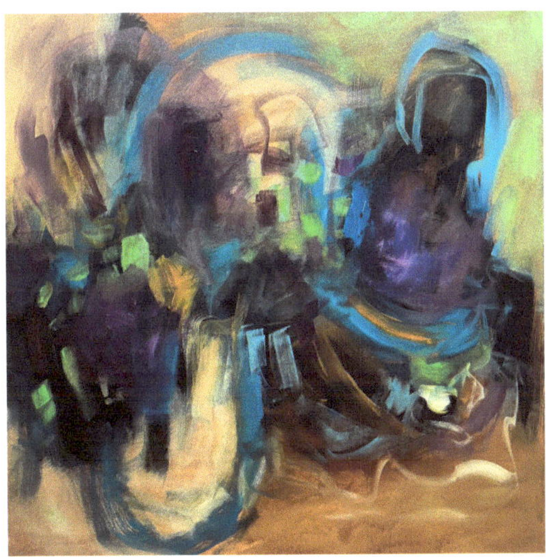

Stage 2

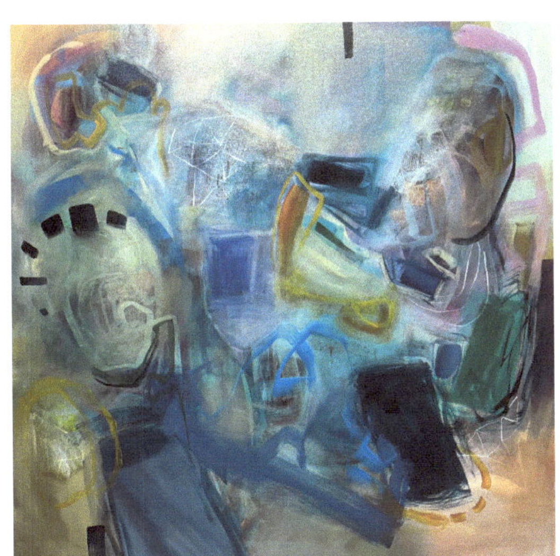

Stage 3

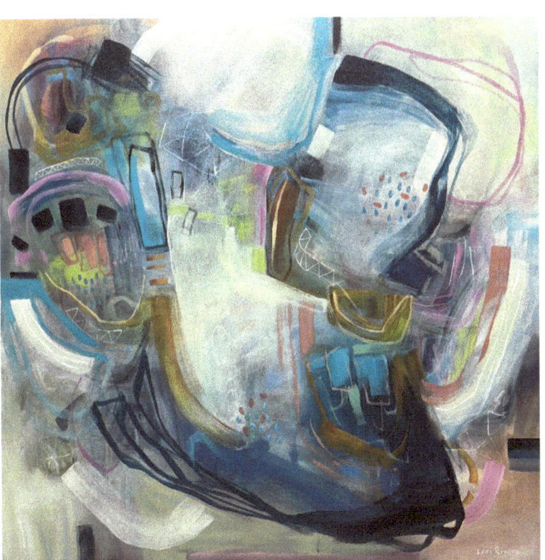

Stage 4 - final stage

How to Begin a Painting

The most effective way to show you how to begin an abstract acrylic painting is to share video demos. You can go to my Bitly page below for a link to all videos or visit the individual videos.

https://bit.ly/m/LoriRivera

Real-Time Abstract Painting Demo
https://bit.ly/AreYouReadyForItDemo

It Takes Two to Tango - How to Start an Abstract Painting
https://bit.ly/ItTakesTwoDemo

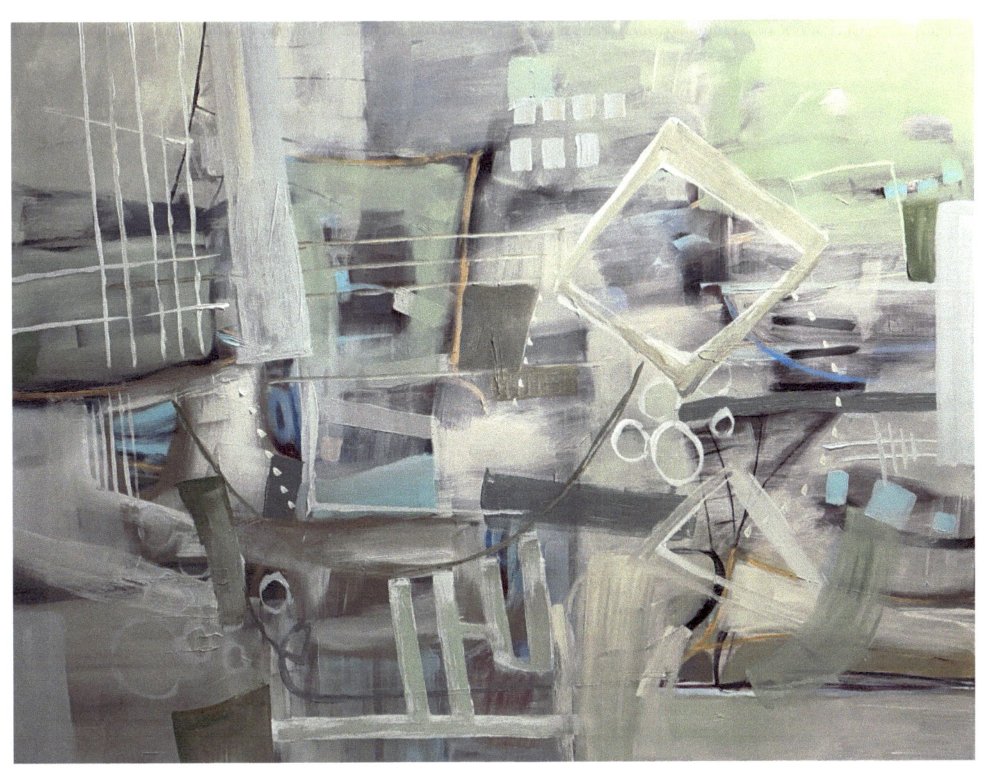

Soft Geometry
36x48 acrylic on canvas

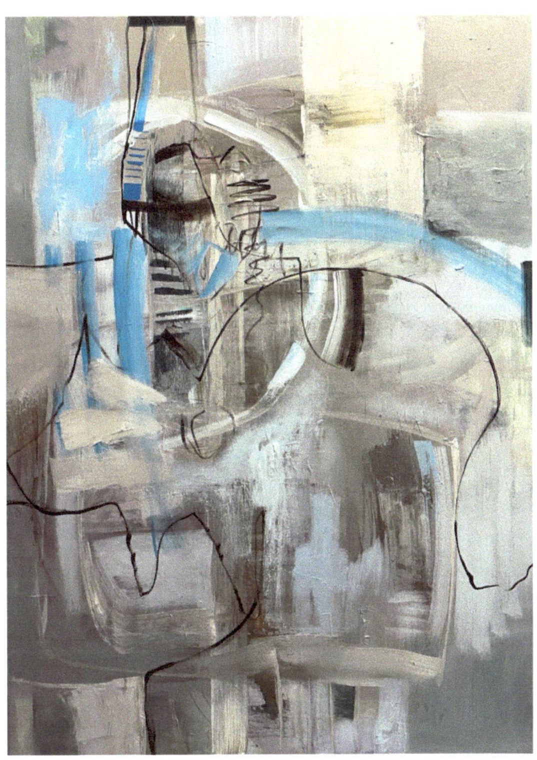

Traces of the Unspoken
40x30 acrylic on canvas

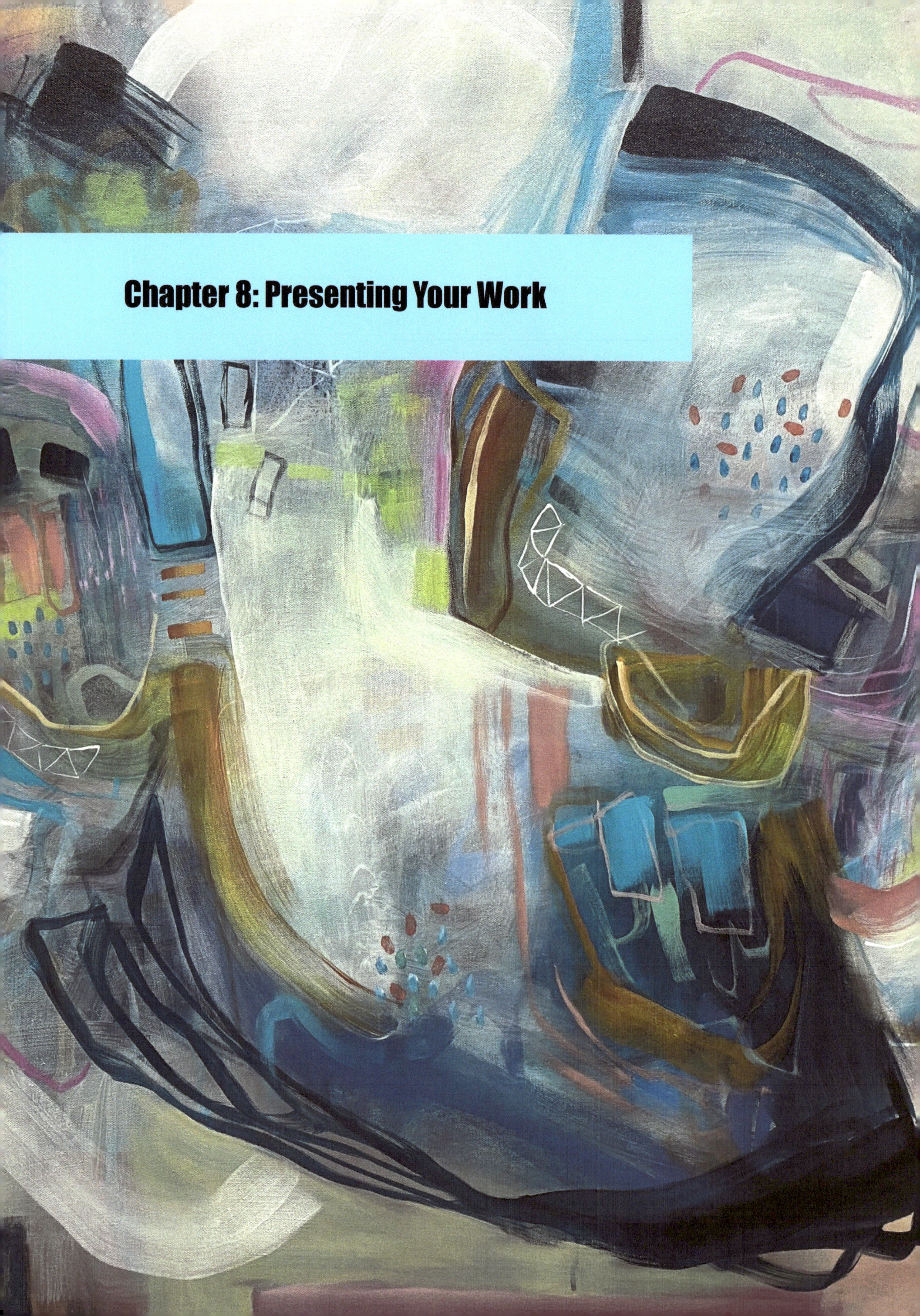

Chapter 8: Presenting Your Work

Presenting Your Work

This chapter is twofold. I'll talk both about how to prepare your work to get it ready to sell, and also give you some ideas for submitting to galleries. You may not feel ready to sell your work yet, but I'm including this information in anticipation that you will eventually want to sell your work.

In this chapter, I share with you several ways of presenting your pieces – framed, unframed, and on an easel. With the no frame option, you paint the edges of your canvas to finish it off. If you prefer your paintings unframed or you frame them yourself, you'll need to wire them. If you don't like doing this part, you can pay a frame shop to wire your pieces for you.

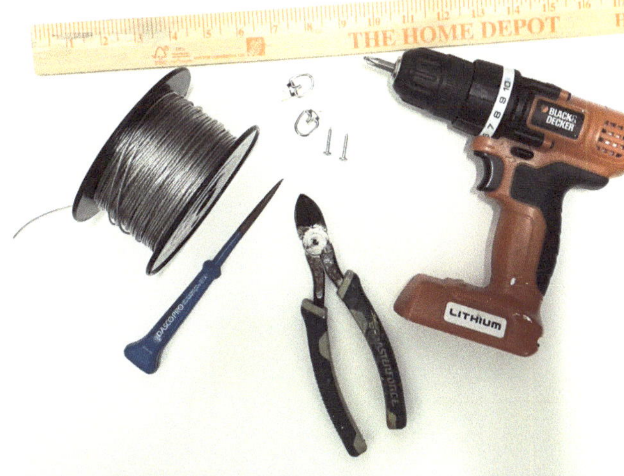

Tools Needed for Wiring

- Ruler
- Picture hanging wire
- Awl
- Wire cutters
- Two D-rings
- Two screws
- Drill

Wiring a Painting (as opposed to a sawtooth hanger)

After you put hours, days, or more of effort into a painting, you will want to properly wire it for hanging. Not only does it look more professional, paintings hang better when they are wired. In the next few pages, I have included step-by-step instructions on how to wire a painting.

In this example, I use D-rings, but you can also use eye screws. D-rings are what most galleries require so if you think you will want to show in a gallery, go ahead and use d-rings.

You can get coated picture wire that holds up to 30 pounds or more, which is what I use, and I'm probably just being extra cautious because even large canvases I've worked with don't weigh that much. Be sure to get coated picture wire as it wraps nicely and you and your client are also less likely to get poked by the wire. The coated picture wire looks more professional also. Wire that holds up to 30 pounds will be strong enough for most of your canvases. If you're ever unsure, weigh your painting and use the proper wire for that weight.

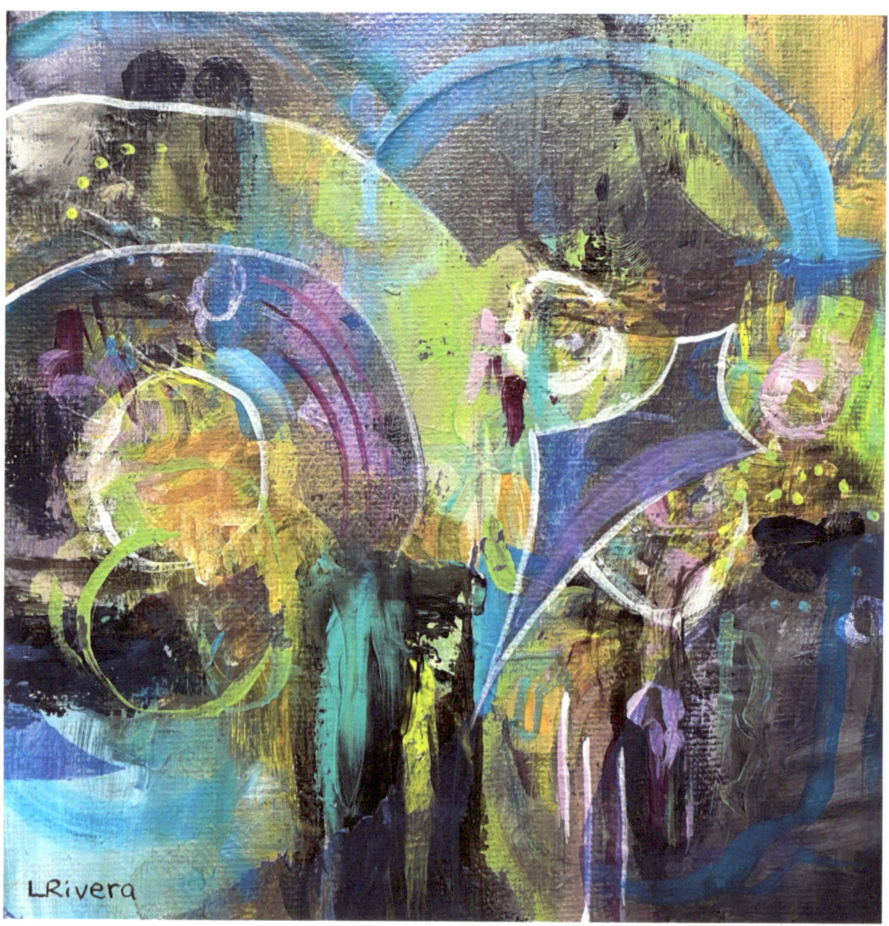

Blowing Bubbles
6x6 acrylic on canvas panel

Wiring an Artwork

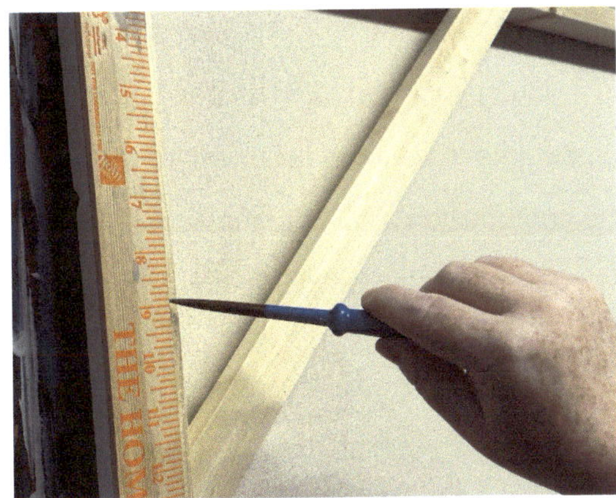

Step 1: Measure 1/3 of the way down from the edge of the painting and use your awl to press a small hole.

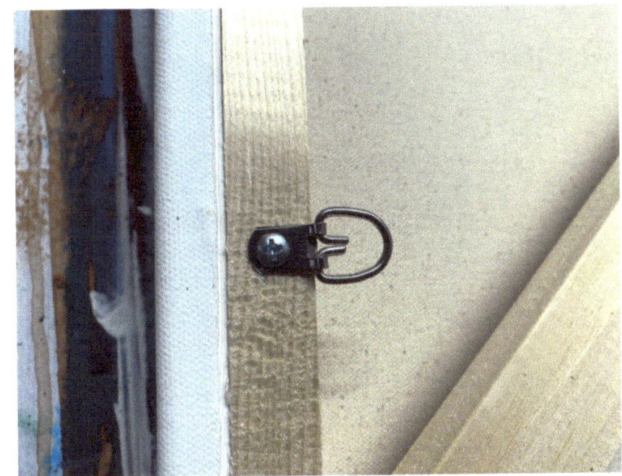

Step 2: Drill the d-ring in to the wood of the canvas where you made a hole with the awl.

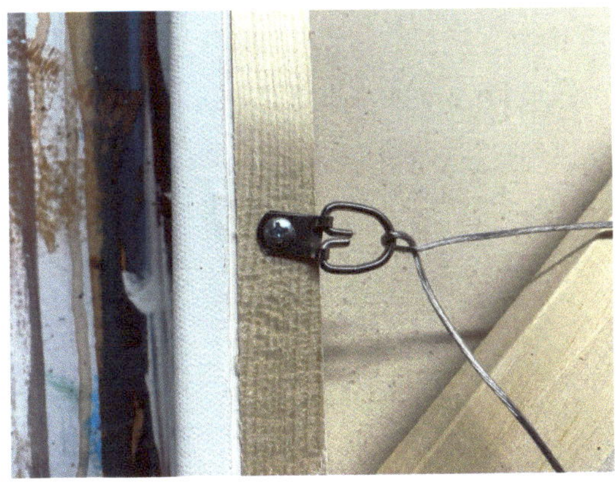

Step 3: Thread the tail of the wire through both d-rings. Take each tail over and under and pull tight. You want your wire between each d-ring to be taut.

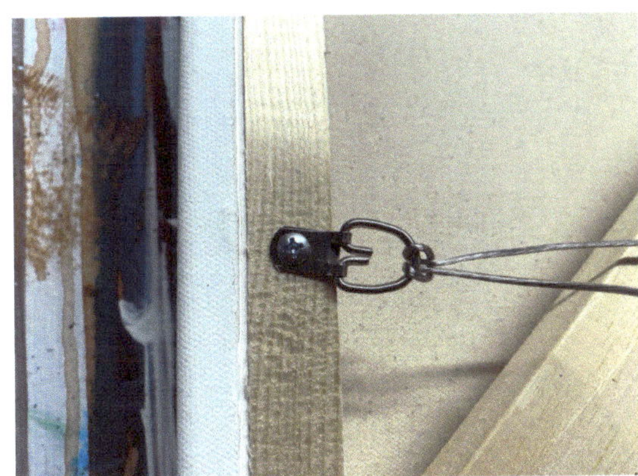

Step 4: String the wire underneath, up and through the loop you just made. Pull tight. Do this with each side.

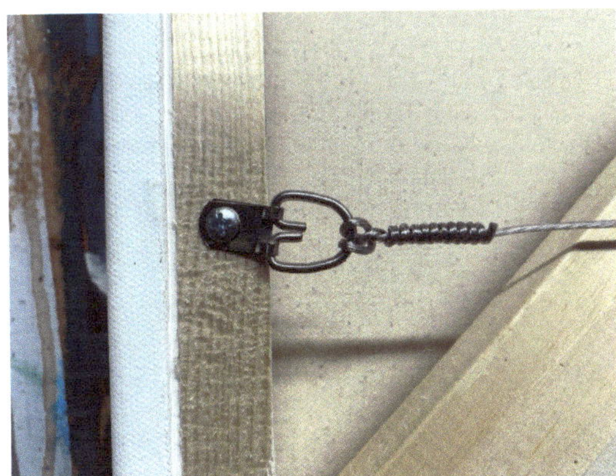

Step 3: Wrap the wire around itself perpendicularly about 10 times. Then cut the tail.

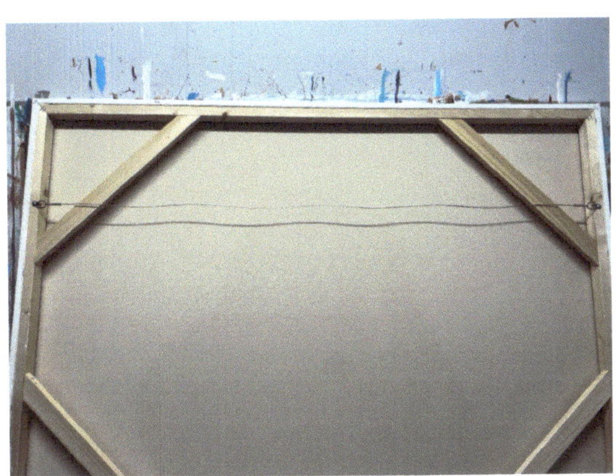

Your final wiring should look something like this.

Painting the Edges

Especially if you're not going to frame your pieces, I recommend painting your edges. They can be painted a solid color, but I have become accustomed to wrapping the composition around to the edges, as shown. This way of finishing off your pieces really gives them a polished look.

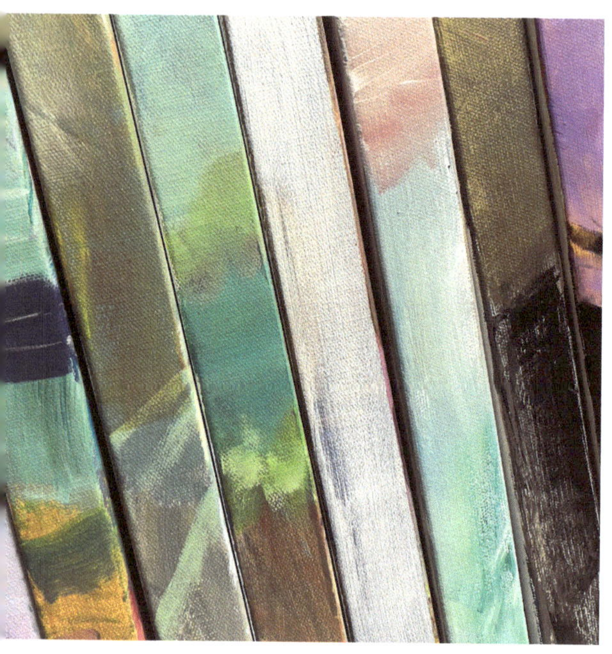
Edges of finished paintings

There are two ways you can do this. You can paint the edges as you go along or you can paint the edges after you finish your piece. Of course, it's much easier as you go along, because if you wait, then you have to mix colors to match. Remember Chapter Four where I talked about using a limited palette? Your limited palette will help in identifying the colors you need to mix for the edges.

Framing

If you paint the edges of your pieces as shown previously, there's no need to frame them. If you like the look of frames, the best option is to have your paintings framed at a professional frame shop. Also, if you know you will frame your pieces, you're better off using traditional profile (.75" deep canvas instead of the deeper ones) canvases, because you'll have more framing options.

You'll want to use open frames for your works on canvas. This allows the paintings to breathe. Open frames are frames without the glass so nothing is covering up your work.

Wait about a week before you frame a piece. Even

acrylic pieces may not be totally dry even if they are dry to the touch. It's always best to let your paintings dry for about a week, and maybe longer if the paint is thick.

DIY Framing

If you like the looks of frames, but can't afford professional framing, you can frame your pieces on your own if you use standard size frames, such as 8x10, 11x14, and 16x20. Just purchase your ready-made frames somewhere like Michael's or a local frame shop, buy some foam rabbet tape, and some offset clips. You'll add a strip of rabbet tape to the inside groove of all four sides of the frame before slipping your canvas inside the frame. This protects your painting rather than placing it directly against the frame. Place your canvas in the frame. Then hold the canvas in place by adding offset clips on all four sides. You may need more than one on each side. Offset clips come in different sizes, so be sure to get the size you need.

If you're framing canvas panels, they're even easier. Just take the glass out of a ready-made store bought frame, line the inside groove with rabbet tape, slip canvas panel in, then attach the back of the frame.

With all this being said, the best way to insure your paintings will be preserved for years to come is to get them professionally framed by a framer who does preservation framing. This will give you peace of mind that your work will last for hundreds of years.

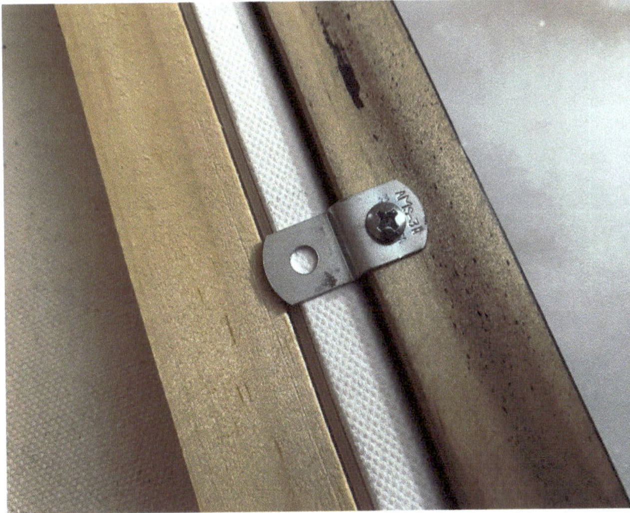

Offset Clip

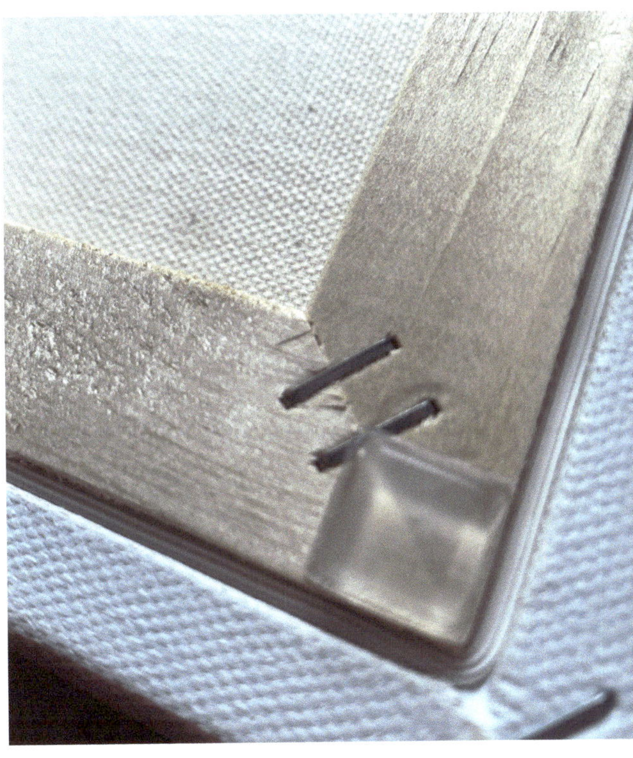

Also consider investing in some clear adhesive bumper pads, as shown in the picture above. You can place one on each bottom corner and they'll help prevent your piece from sliding on the wall. You can use these on both framed and unframed canvases.

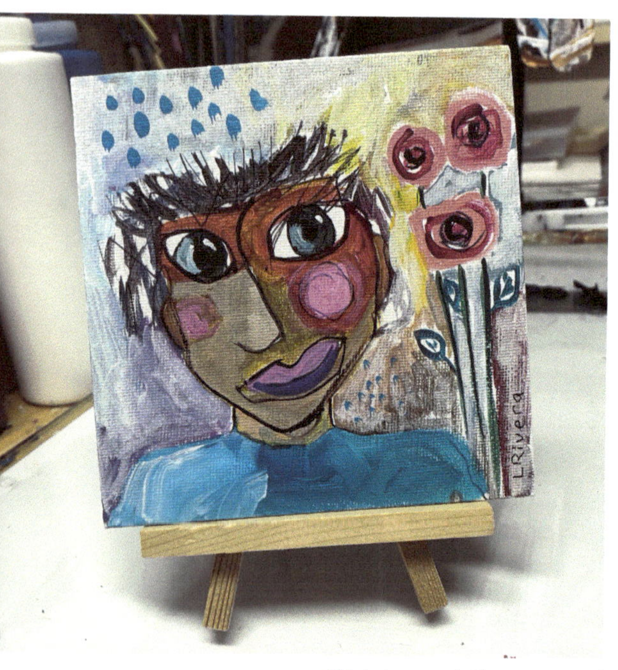

Miniature painting on easel

Using Easels for Display

You can also display your work on tabletop easels, which come in a variety of sizes and designs. Some are ornate and others are very simple. I often use easels for my small works on canvas panels and here is one of my miniature funky abstract portraits placed on a miniature easel. I'm so excited about this way of displaying small pieces.

Signing Your Artwork

An artist signature is the final stamp on each piece created that says to the world "I am finished with this painting, and I approve it." But have you ever really given much thought to how you sign your paintings? I have changed my artist signature throughout the years and I think I've finally settled on a signature. I sign my paintings as LRivera. Many would argue that I should include my first name spelled out, and believe me, I've almost changed it numerous times, but for some reason I like it as is, mainly because it's short. The longer the signature, the more I think it detracts from the painting, drawing, or other piece of art. Do you want a cursive signature, a printed signature, just your initials, or a shape as your signature?

Try to stay away from using a signature that looks like how you would sign a check. This is your art, not a check. That's one reason I use a printed signature, but I've seen artists get pretty creative with cursive signatures, and they look very nice.

Be consistent with your artist signature. What I mean by this is always use the same medium for your signature that you used in your art piece. Using the same medium and a color from your painting for your signature helps make your painting look polished. My exception to this rule is when I paint miniatures (what I consider to be 6x6 or smaller). It's more difficult to sign my name with paint on these since they are so small. In this case, sometimes I use a black archival artist pen and sign very small.

Try not to make your signature too large because it will detract from the painting. On the other hand, don't make it too small or people won't even notice it. And if someone loves your painting and wants to know who painted it, how disappointing it would be for them to not see your signature. Look at the signatures of successful artists while you come up with your own signature.

Use a color you used in your painting to sign your piece. Doing this helps provide evidence that you painted the piece, if it is ever in question in the future.

Leave extra room below and to the side of your signature. You never know who may want to frame your piece, even if you have gallery wrapped edges. If someone wants to frame your piece, have you left enough room around your signature so that it doesn't get covered up by the frame? I try to leave at least a half inch to the side of and below my signature, unless it's a smaller piece in which I have to leave less space.

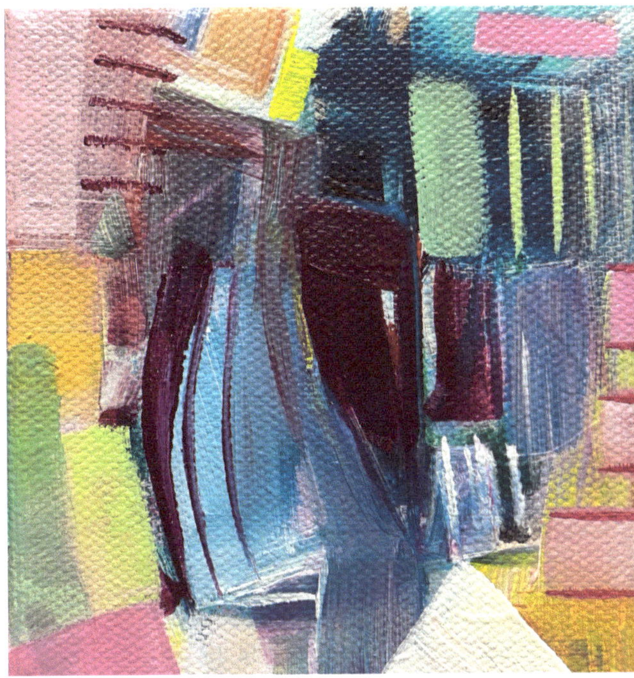

Watcha Gonna Do Now
4x4 acrylic on canvas

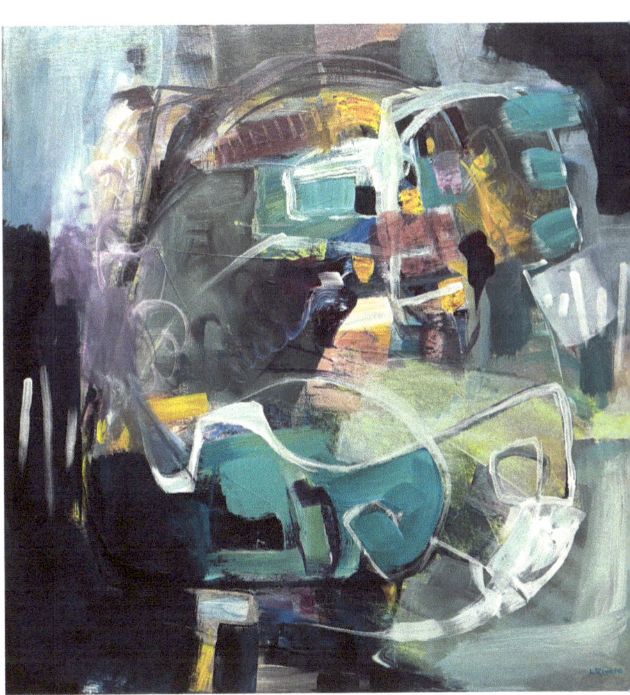

Hangin' On
24x24 acrylic on canvas

Presenting Your Work to Galleries

Taking Photos of Your Work

For most purposes, you can just take photos of your work with your phone. The cameras on phones do a pretty good job. These photos will be fine for sharing your work on social media or your website.

You want to crop the background out of a picture like this, as shown below.

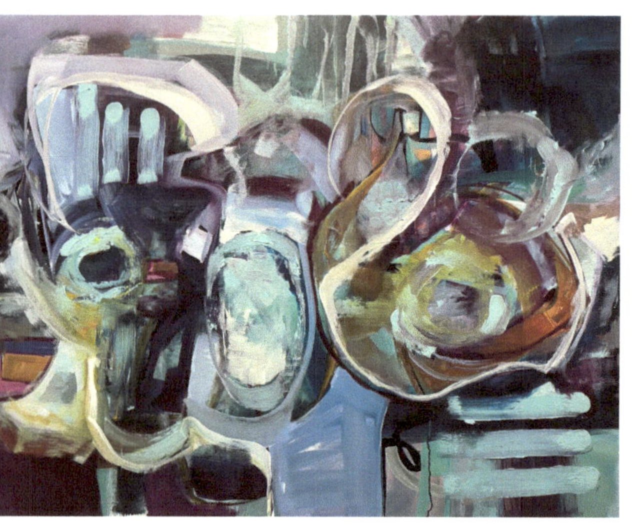

See how much better this looks in comparison to the photo above.

The only time you need high resolution photos with a DSLR camera is if you're going to have prints made of your work. You can also scan your pieces to get high resolution as long as your pieces are small enough to scan.

When taking photos of your work, they look best if you crop out the background, especially for your website. The only time I'd leave the background in is if you're showing the scale of your work.

Submitting to Galleries

You'll always want to crop out the background of your photos when submitting to galleries. High resolution photos are always the best to submit, but honestly sending pictures I take with my phone have worked fine for this purpose.

When submitting to galleries, it's best to submit cohesive pieces instead of say, five pieces in all different styles. Galleries like to see that you've developed a strong artistic voice.

If you want to submit to a gallery, first try to determine if the gallery is a good fit. If a gallery's focus is on traditional landscapes, then your abstract work would not fit in with their mix. With that being said, galleries do like to take on artists whose work looks different than anything they currently show. If you're submitting to an abstract art gallery and your work looks very similar to an artist they already have, your chances aren't as good. But, you'll never know the answer until you actually submit your work.

Also find out how to contact them as most galleries have a process for taking submissions. Some have you email them information, some have online forms, and others may have different submission guidelines.

It's never a good idea to show up at a gallery unannounced with your work. Not only is this disrespectful of their time schedule, you're putting them on the spot.

If you're looking for a gallery to represent you, Google is a good way to look for galleries. I also recommend visiting the galleries in person to get a feel for the vibe.

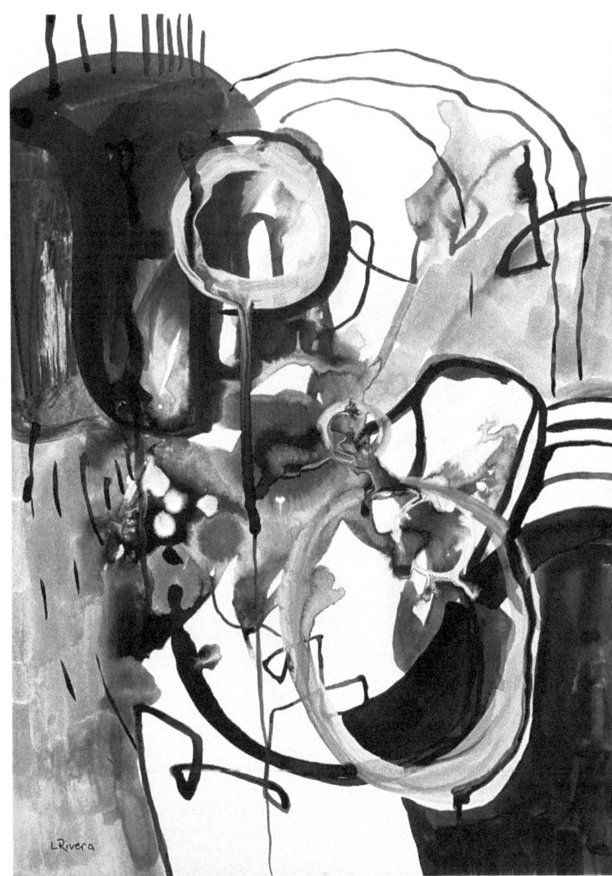

Intimate Conversation
12x9 black ink on bristol paper

Common things galleries ask for is your artist statement, curriculum vitae (CV or artist resume), and your exhibition history, along with pictures of your work. Keep all this information at your fingertips. I keep each of these as a file in Google Drive.

Keep track of every show or art-related event you're a part of and put it on your CV. I even list Artist talks, shows I've curated, and grants I've received on my CV. If you have a college degree, but it's not in art, I'd put your education last, as it's not as relevant to your art career.

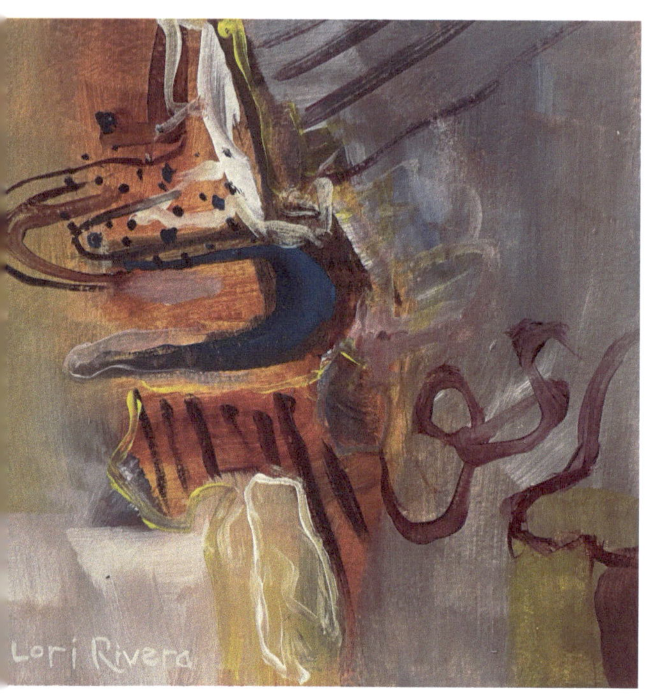

Untitled
6x6 acrylic on paper

If you're not necessarily looking for gallery representation, but want to submit to individual shows, Café (callforentry.org) is the place to use. They list local, regional, national, and international shows you can apply to. There's almost always an entry fee, usually between $20-$40. I wrote this book in 2025, so if you're reading this book years later, it's probably higher. There are also grant opportunities listed on occasion.

You may also live in a city where there are some galleries that offer group shows. They may or may not list those opportunities on Call for Entry. For this reason, be sure to reach out and connect with them or follow their website and social media for information about shows.

Packaging Your Paintings to Ship

Supplies Needed

- Glassine paper
- Bubble wrap
- Acid free artist tape
- Packing tape
- Cardboard corners
- Foam Board
- "Fragile" sticker

To ship your piece, wrap your paintings with glassine paper and secure the paper with acid free tape. Not only is glassine paper acid free, it won't stick to your painting either.

Add cardboard corners to all four corners and attach

them with packing tape. I purchased my corners from Amazon.

Make sure you include a business card and any other necessary documents.

Then wrap the entire painting with several layers of bubble wrap with the flat side touching on the inside.

Sandwich the art between two pieces of foam board (a little larger than the piece).

Next place the painting in a box and add bubble wrap as necessary. Add a fragile sticker to the outside. And always package your art yourself. If you have the carrier (FedEx or UPS) package it, you'll end up paying a fortune.

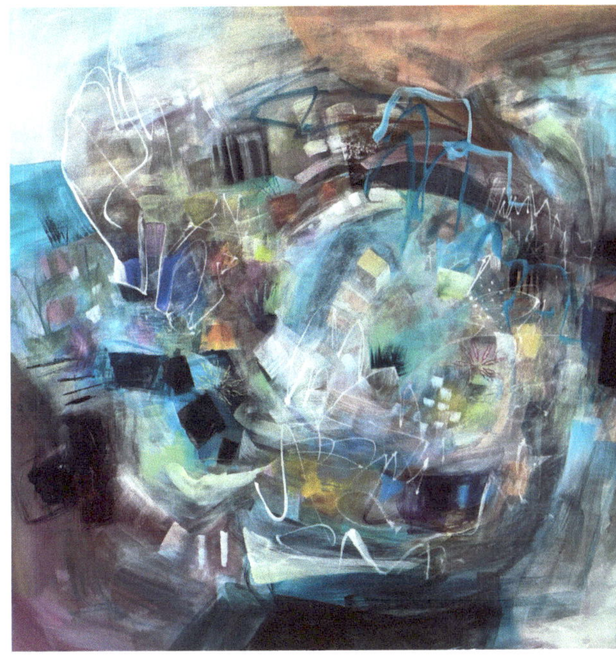

Open-Ended
20x20 acrylic on canvas

TIP: You can make any color more transparent (to allow the underneath layer to show through) by adding a medium to it. I use Nova Color varnish to create transparent colors. I mix it straight in with the paint. In the painting above you can see many transparent layers.

I used to use glazing liquid but found the varnish works just as well, and I can order it by the gallon.

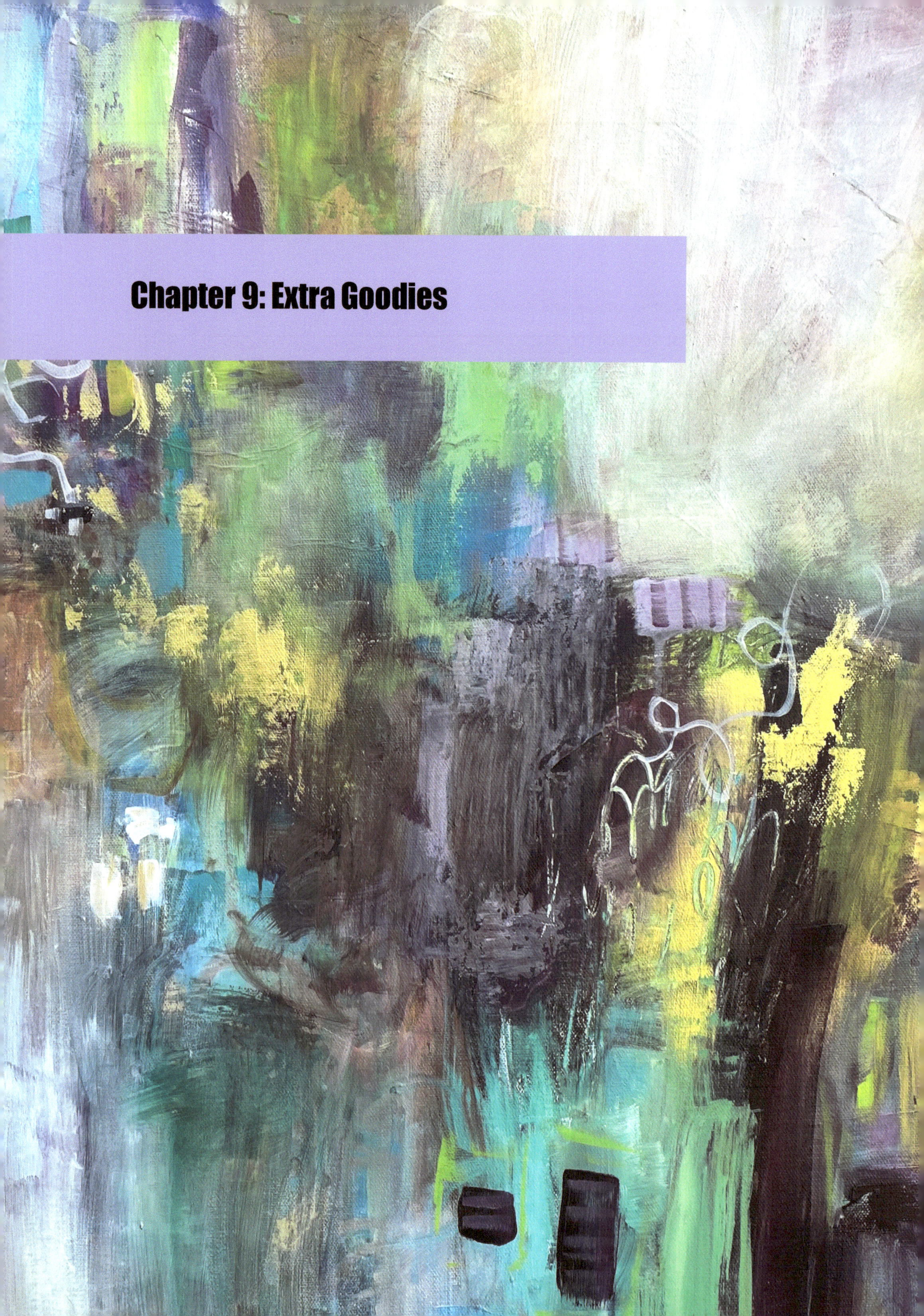

Chapter 9: Extra Goodies

In this chapter, I share things that I think are important that didn't fit into any of the other chapters.

How to Unleash Your Creativity

Try a Variation of Something You're Already Doing

The best example I can think of from my own creative practice is when I paint with my non-dominant hand. I find my work is much looser when I try using my non-dominant hand because I have less control over that hand. It really produces a different look entirely. Sometimes I will just do this with a couple of parts of my painting. Other times, I won't do it at all. But if I'm feeling stuck, sometimes I'll use my non-dominant hand. Think about how you might do something a bit differently in your creative process. Sometimes just a slight variation will produce vastly different results.

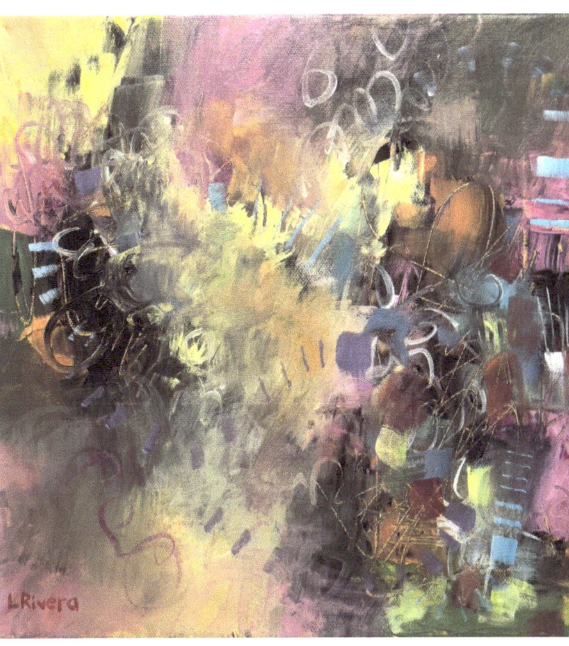

Pink Crush
12x12 acrylic on canvas

Try Something New

A couple of years ago, I took some still life painting classes. I'd never really done still life painting in the past so it was all pretty new to me. What I found is that I could take the still life techniques I was learning and apply them to my abstracts. Not only that, but when we try new things, we create new pathways in our brains. According to Very Well Mind (verywellmind.com), "Modern research has demonstrated that the brain continues to create new neural pathways and alter existing ones in order to adapt to new experiences, learn new information, and create new memories."

Trying out a new hobby -- sewing, writing, painting,

cooking, or something else -- is a great way of trying new things. Or you can simply try something new within a hobby or profession you already have as I did with the still life painting. Many times, something new can inform another creative task.

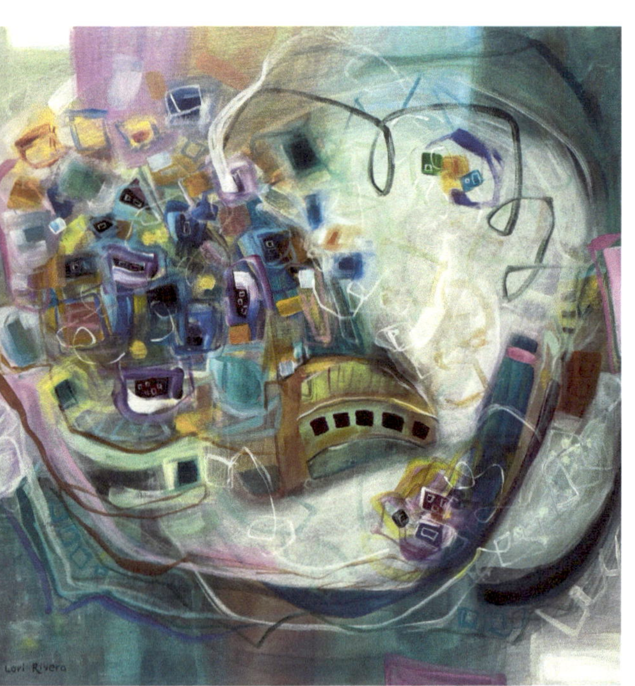

Path of Least Resistance
24x24 acrylic on canvas

Look for Inspiration Around You

I'm a firm believer that nothing is created 100 percent out of thin air. In other words, I think inspiration for projects is usually found around us. Many artists find inspiration from other artists, and the same goes for writers and other creative professionals. Maybe you like the colors in a shirt and use those colors as your color palette in your next painting. Maybe you're inspired by the architecture in a small town and apply that architectural style to your painting of a street of homes based on your imagination.

Practice Creativity Daily

Wherever you're using your creativity, make it a daily practice. Try to take on a small project daily. I believe daily creative practice maximizes your creativity, and I compare creativity to learning a new language. It really needs daily attention, and if given that attention, it will become so ingrained in you that you'll eventually bring out your natural-born creativity.

Find Your Creative Tribe

I believe creatives thrive the most when they can feed off the energy and are inspired by other creative types. If you knit, find a knitting group to join. If you write, join a writer's group. As for me, I have a small group of artists I talk to nearly every day. Sometimes we get together just to spend time together and enjoy each others company, and other times we actually get together to paint. We talk nearly every day to bounce ideas off of one another about projects we are working on and we share business advice with each other. I don't know what I'd do without my artist friends! They're definitely my tribe.

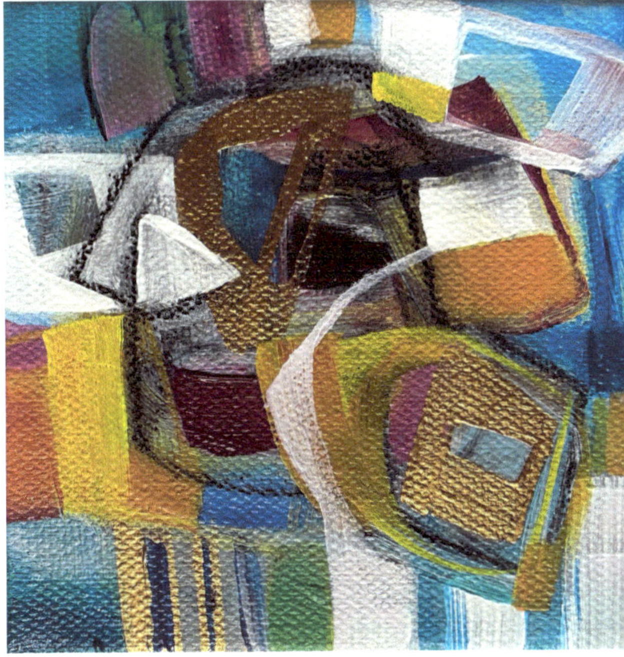

I Still Remember When
4x4 acrylic on canvas

Recharge

Make sure you have time each day to relax and recharge, whatever that might look like for you. Take a half an hour to rest with your eyes closed while listening to music, take time to read, or make a refreshing dessert. Creativity is kind of like exercise. You need to do it often, but you need to take breaks as well. Creativity requires a lot of energy, which means we do need to recharge at times. Just like a runner needs breaks to drink water, creativity requires time to rest.

Additionally, sometimes we need to take a break from our creative work and recharge so that we can come back to it later with fresh eyes. If I'm running into roadblocks in my creative practice, simply walking away from it for an hour, or even a couple days, can have a huge impact on my work when I come back to it.

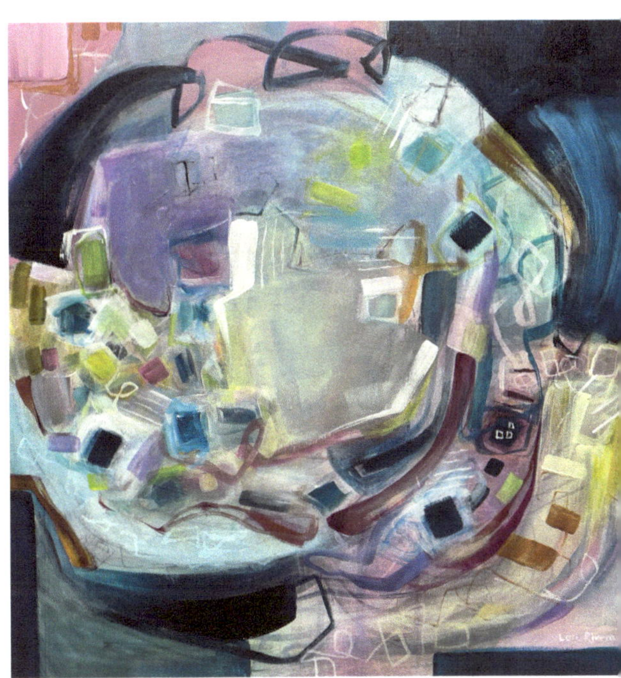

Closer
24x24 acrylic on canvas

Change Your Routine

It can be hard enough to figure out when our most creative time of the day is, and it does seem that most people have an ideal time to create each day. The best time for me to create is at night.

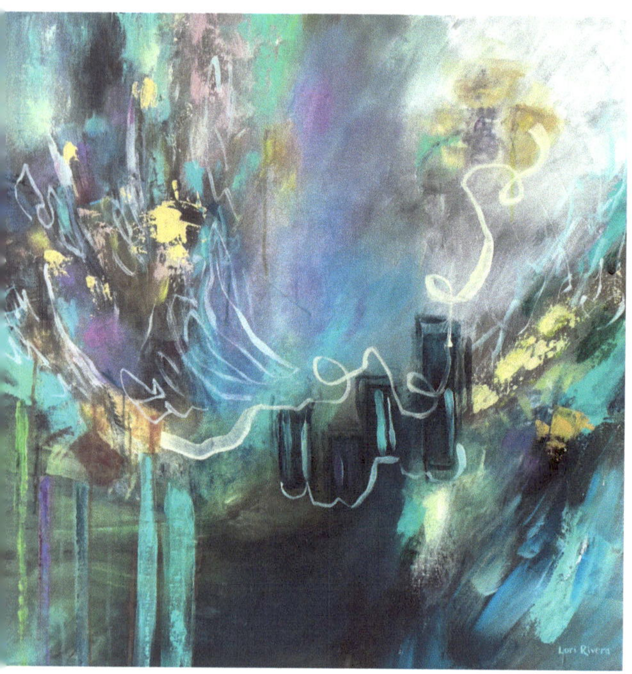

Duh Duh Dun Dun
24x24 acrylic on canvas

I do believe if we make minor changes to our routine (while only changing one variable at a time), we can determine our optimum creative space and time to create.

What could changing your routine look like? For me, it would be taking my paints outside and painting outdoors (plein air) instead of confining myself to my studio. It could also be changing the time of day I paint. Or it could even be changing the music I listen to while I paint.

The variables that you test can really be absolutely anything and are endless. It could even be measuring your creativity with different hours of sleep. Do you need 6, 7, 8, or another number of hours of sleep to reach your maximum creative potential? These are all valid variables and I'm sure you can think of more you can experiment with.

Selecting + Hanging Your Artwork

Selecting artwork for your space is a very personal journey as everyone has their own likes and dislikes when it comes to artwork. My best advice is to hang artwork that you absolutely love. You're going to be living with it so it should be something you're totally in love with.

Statement Pieces

I'm a firm believer that every room should have a statement piece -- the main piece of the room that is the focal point. Just as most pieces of artwork have a focal point, I think your rooms should too. Usually statement pieces are the largest piece in the room. After your statement piece, then you can fill in other areas of the room with smaller pieces.

Hanging Artwork

The number one tip I have for you is to hang your artwork at what would be eye level for the average height person. This is especially important for businesses who serve the public. In your own home, you'll probably want to simply hang your art according to the height of the people who live in the home.

The type of screw or nail in hanging your piece is also important because you want to make sure the artwork doesn't slip off the wall. For this reason, use nails and screws that have heads, which will serve as an anchor for the wire. If you have plaster walls, you'll want to drill a hole and use a screw. For drywall, the best way is to hammer a picture hanger to the wall with a nail. If you are hanging a heavy piece, you may even need to use a drywall anchor to prevent it from falling.

Arrangement

Just as in composing the elements of a piece of artwork, I think multiple pieces always look best if they are hung in odd numbers, as shown to the right. If you do hang an even number of pieces, they might look better staggered.

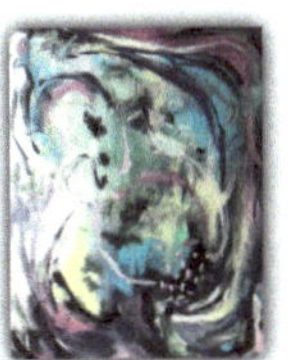
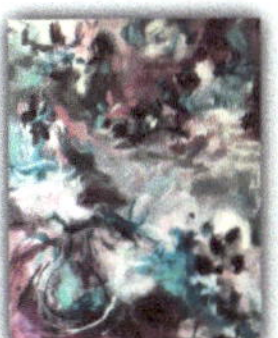
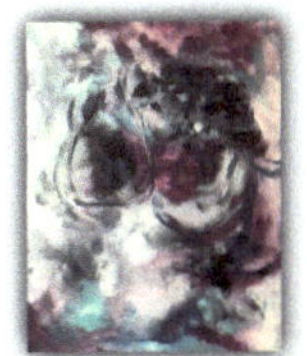
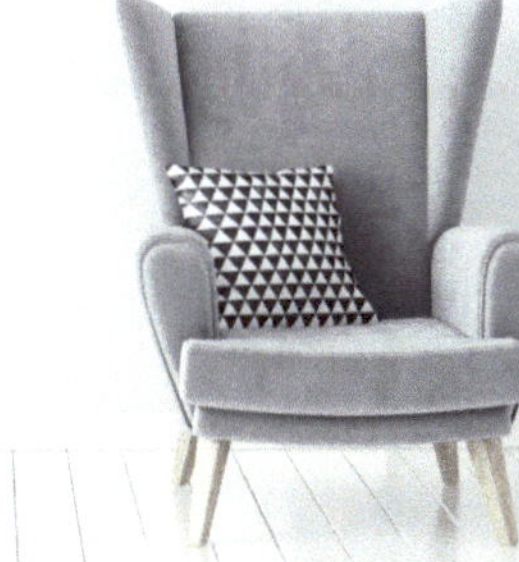

Hang an odd number of pieces together

Other Tidbits

Titling Your Work

Always try to assign good titles to your work. If you painted a pink rose, for example, try not to title it "pink rose," although I have been guilty of this myself. Try something unique and figurative, such as "First Day of Summer." Literal titles can be boring. Try not to use "Untitled" as a title either. Giving your piece a title will make it appear that it is an important part of your work and will elevate it in the eyes of the collector.

Look at Your Paintings From Afar

Always take a look at your piece across the room periodically while painting it to see if your painting looks good from afar. Sometimes paintings look great close up, but not far away, and ideally they should look good from anywhere. A good rule to follow is to make sure your painting looks good from two feet away, six feet away, and all the way across the room.

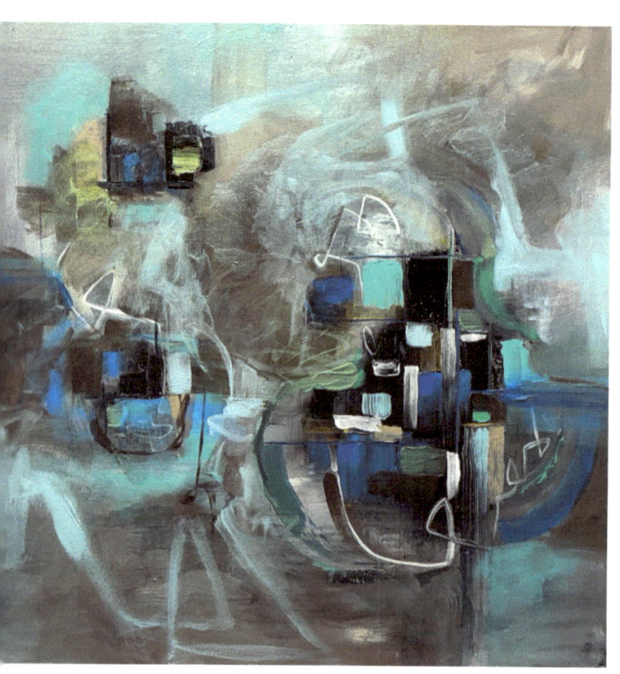

Playing in Rain Puddles
24x24 acrylic on canvas

Imperfection Can Be Beauty

Learn to find beauty in imperfection. Lines don't have to be straight. Circles don't have to be perfectly round. Using organic shapes is what I prefer, but you may find you want your work to be tighter, and that's okay. Everyone is different. But learning to find beauty in imperfection can be so freeing.

Work Fast

Work fast and rely on intuition to guide your next brushstroke. Working fast doesn't allow much time for thinking about the painting. It also helps prevent you from overworking a piece. If you are trying to achieve a looser style, working fast will help.

Rotate Your Work

Rotate your piece in all directions to see which way you like it best before signing your name. You may even want to rotate pieces throughout the painting process. Go ahead and turn it upside down, and start painting it that way.

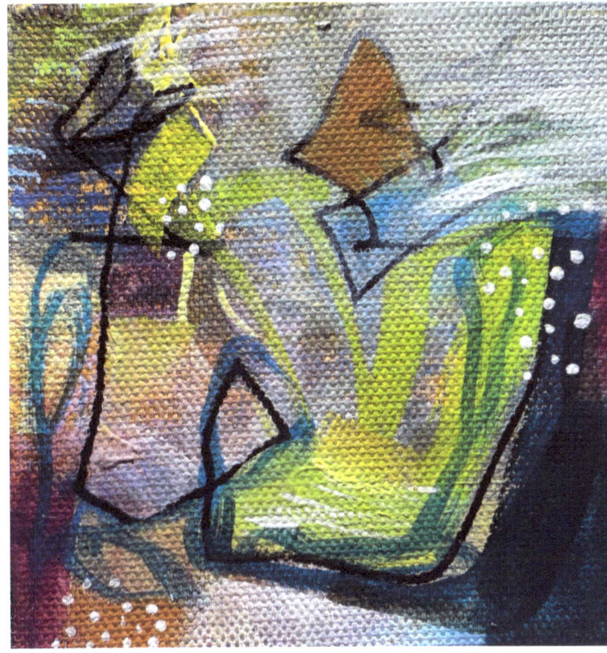

Color Splash No. 1
4x4 acrylic on canvas

Exercises

Create Small Pieces from a Larger Piece

This is a fun optional project you can try. Get a big piece of paper and place it on the floor. Paint it abstractly however you wish. When you finish, cut the paper into smaller pieces. You can now mount the pieces with heavy gel medium onto pieces of wood. You can also make miniature diptychs and triptychs out of the pieces. A diptych is two pieces made to hang together, and a triptych is three pieces.

30 Day Painting Challenge

I created the painting prompts list on the following page so you can practice things learned in this book while using your imagination. This is also good practice if you are wanting to take commissions. These are pretty open prompts, but it is a step in the right direction for preparing you for commissions. Clients will have all kinds of requests, from color and composition to the overall feel of the piece. I usually steer away from painting abstract commissions because they're so subjective.

30 Day Painting Prompts

1. Energetic
2. Raw
3. Fearless
4. Dots
5. Slow
6. Circles
7. Quiet
8. Mirrored
9. Magical
10. Turquoise
11. 3D
12. Complementary
13. Open
14. Bold
15. Dark
16. Closed
17. Light
18. Analogous
19. Squares
20. Splatter
21. Shadows
22. Orange
23. Repeat
24. Sadness
25. Loud
26. Harmonious
27. Seasons
28. Fast
29. Stripes
30. Calm

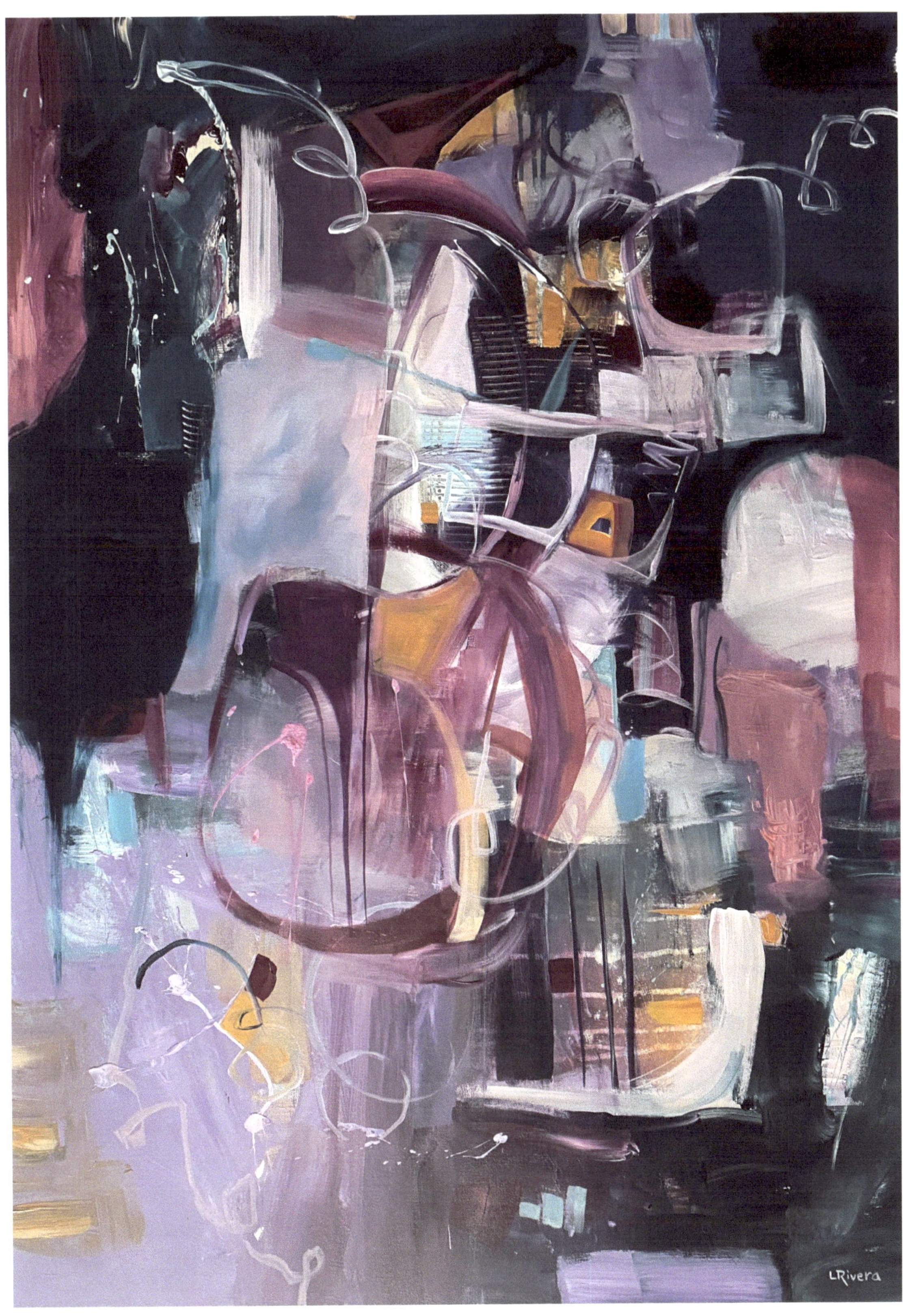

But You Came Along, 48x36 acrylic on canvas

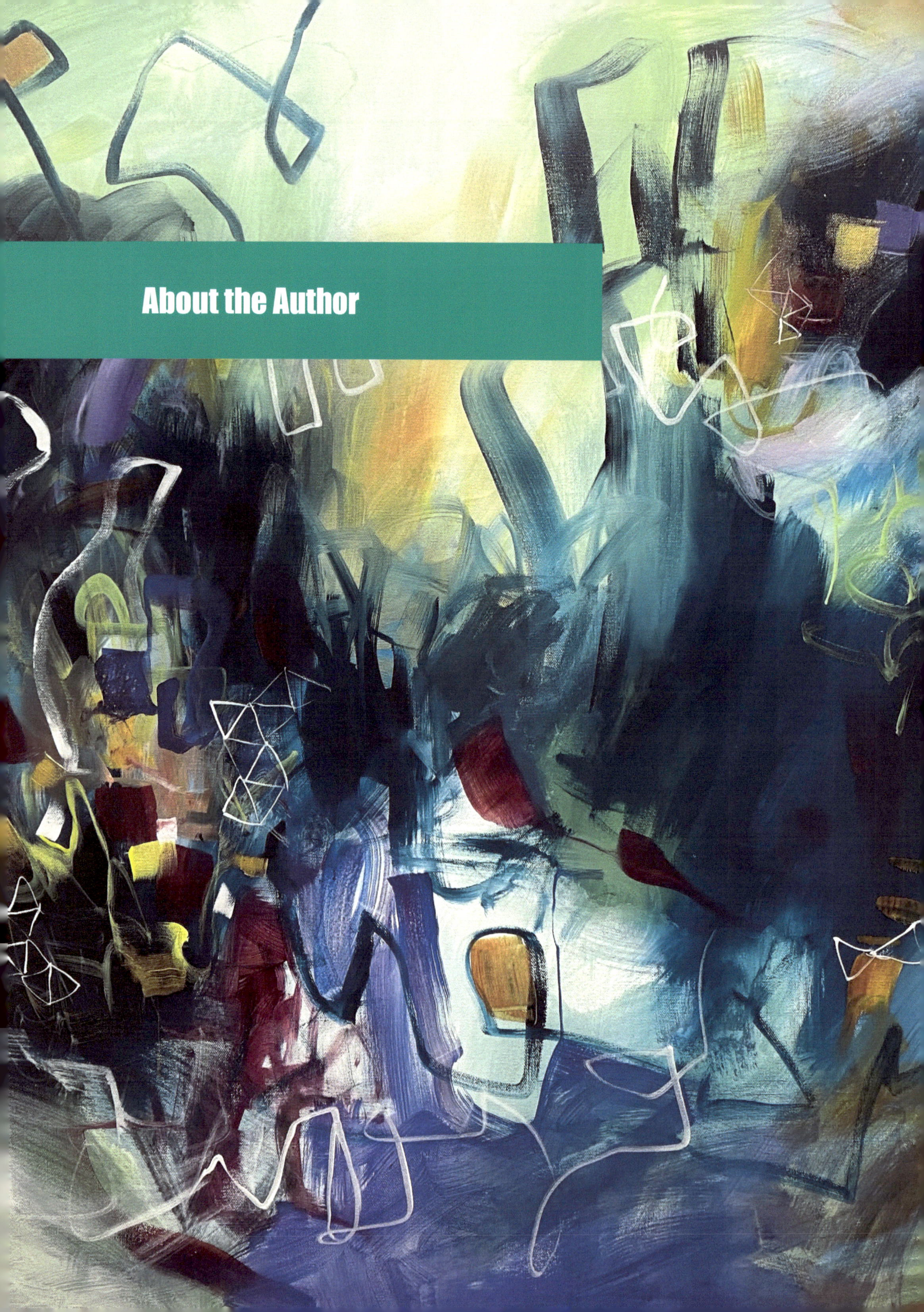

About the Author

BIO

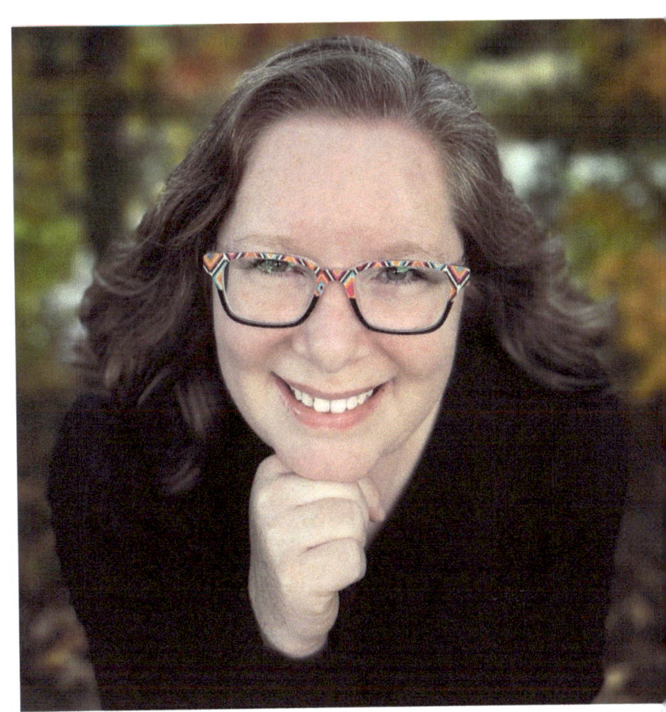

Although I chose to study business in college instead of attending art school, my passion for art never left me. In my late 30s, while working as the Director of a nonprofit peer-run recovery center, I was surrounded by passionate artists in the Arts Empowerment program. Their creative spark reignited my young adulthood dream of becoming an artist. Returning to art after years away felt like a breath of fresh air. It not only filled a missing piece in my life but also improved my mental health and connected me to a supportive art community.

In addition to peer mental health and nonprofit management, I've also worked in web development and marketing. I currently live in Evansville, Indiana with my husband, daughter, and our three cats. When I'm not painting in my home studio, I enjoy spending time with friends and family, working a couple days a week at a local frame shop & gallery, and collaborating with fellow artists.

ARTIST STATEMENT

My abstract work is a journey into the subconscious, a visual exploration of the intuitive mind. Each piece is a reflection of a moment in time, unfiltered and unrestrained, where the brush and canvas become extensions of my inner self.

In my process, I embrace the unpredictability and freedom of abstract expression. There are no preconceived plans or sketches; instead, I allow my instincts to guide me, letting each stroke and color

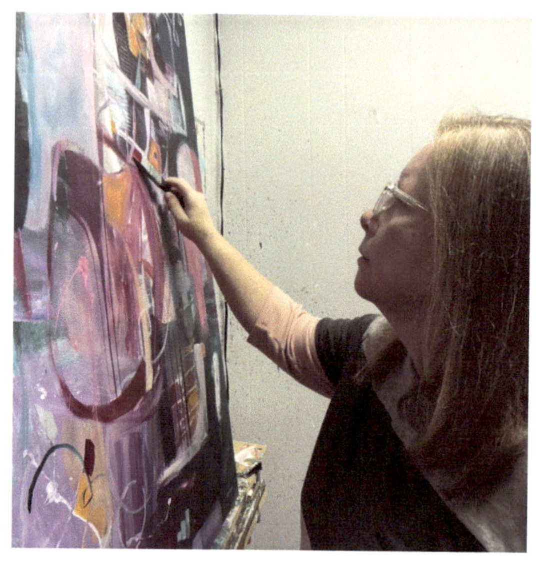

develop organically. This approach not only brings a sense of immediacy and authenticity to my work but also invites viewers to engage with their interpretations and emotional responses.

My goal is for the viewer to experience strong emotions when viewing my work. I strive to create a mood for the viewer, however she may interpret the work.

Best wishes in your abstract art painting journey! I'd love to hear from you. I can be reached at loririveraart@gmail.com

www.loririveraart.com

Did you enjoy this book and was it helpful? *Please leave me a review on Amazon, Goodreads, etc.* I would greatly appreciate it!

Courses

Here are a few courses I've designed. If you're interested in any of them, just go to my YouTube at https://bit.ly/LoriRiveraYT

Using Google Sheets to Track the Health of Your Art Business

https://bit.ly/GoogleSheetsForArtists

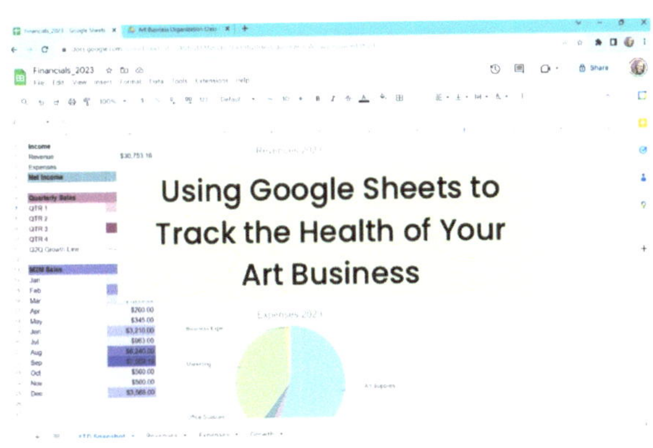

Painting a Cardinal

https://bit.ly/CardinalPainting

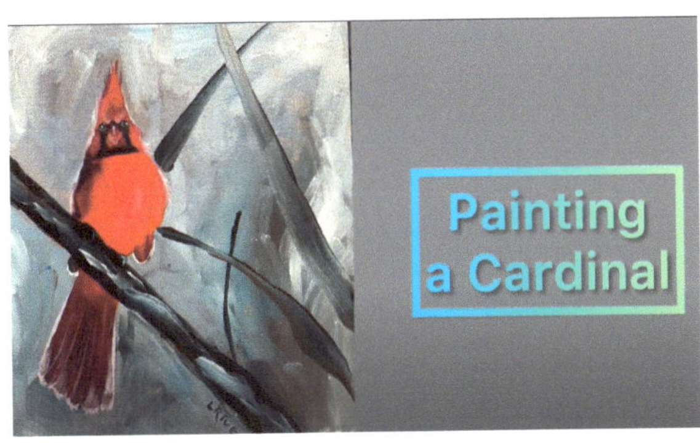

Index

W

www.ingramcontent.com/pod-product-compliance
Ingram Content Group UK Ltd.
Pitfield, Milton Keynes, MK11 3LW, UK
UKHW060106300726
14090UKWH00003B/390

* 9 7 9 8 9 9 9 5 2 8 0 0 1 *